URU™

AGES BEYOND MYST®

Prima's Official Travel Guide

Bryan Stratton

Prima Games
A Division of Random House, Inc.

3000 Lava Ridge Court
Roseville, CA 95661
1-800-733-3000
www.primagames.com

D1300711

URU
AGES BEYOND MYST®
Prima's Official Travel Guide

Product Manager: Jill Hinckley
Project Editor: Carrie Ponseti

Uru, Myst and Cyan are trademarks or registered trademarks of Cyan Worlds, Inc.

All products and characters mentioned in this book are trademarks of their respective companies.

Please be advised that the ESRB rating icons, "EC", "K-A", "E", "T", "M", "AO" and "RP" are copyrighted works and certification marks owned by the Entertainment Software Association and the Entertainment Software Rating Board and may only be used with their permission and authority. Under no circumstances may the rating icons be self-applied or used in connection with any product that has not been rated by the ESRB. For information regarding whether a product has been rated by the ESRB, please call the ESRB at 1-800-771-3772 or visit www.esrb.org. For information regarding licensing issues, please call the ESA at (212) 223-8936. Please note that ESRB ratings only apply to the content of the game itself and does NOT apply to the content of this book.

Important:
Prima Games has made every effort to determine that the information contained in this book is accurate. However, the publisher makes no warranty, either expressed or implied, as to the accuracy, effectiveness, or completeness of the material in this book; nor does the publisher assume liability for damages, either incidental or consequential, that may result from using the information in this book. The publisher cannot provide information regarding game play, hints and strategies, or problems with hardware or software. Questions should be directed to the support numbers provided by the game and device manufacturers in their documentation. Some game tricks require precise timing and may require repeated attempts before the desired result is achieved.

ISBN: 0-7615-4470-4
Library of Congress Catalog Card Number: 2003112037
Printed in the United States of America

04 05 06 JJ 10 9 8 7 6 5 4 3

Acknowledgments
Bryan Stratton would like to thank: Rand Miller, Ryan Miller, and Chris Brandkamp for their hospitality, advice, and comprehensive knowledge of D'ni culture; Terry Coolidge for his technical expertise; Tony Fryman, inventor of the Fry-Man aquarium; and Patti Van Heel for helping to prepare me for the journey. Thanks also to Jennifer Crotteau, Jill Hinckley, and Carrie Ponseti of Prima Games for putting in the necessary long hours and having the willingness to publish such an unconventional guide. Finally, thanks to fellow travelers Stephen Stratton, David Hodgson, Holly Hannam, and Seanbaby (*Myst* fan #1). Join the DRC today!

Contents

URU
AGES BEYOND MYST®
Prima's Official Travel Guide

Dear Valued Customer,

Thank you for purchasing *Uru: Ages Beyond Myst: Prima's Official Travel Guide*. It is our sincere hope that this guide will provide you with as much information as possible about the latest journey through the lost history of the D'ni.

We have been fortunate to have the opportunity to publish this guide at a remarkable time in history. Within the last few years, human explorers from the D'ni Restoration Council (DRC) have not only discovered the lost D'ni city and several of its Ages, but they are preparing to open them to explorers who share their passion for rediscovering this long lost society.

It was our intention to send an author down to D'ni with Dr. Richard Watson of the DRC. However, as you will read in the following pages, our author became sidetracked and proceeded to explore aspects of D'ni life that even the DRC have not fully researched. Despite some initial objections from the DRC, we have decided to publish this guide as a largely unedited transcription of the author's original handwritten journal. The photographs in this guide are the actual photographs taken by the author during his journey, and the comments written along the bottom of the photographs are his own.

While the events contained within this journal border on the fantastic, we would like to reassure our readers that these are the actual experiences of our author. We have seen his photographs, we have heard the voices and sounds captured on his tape recorder, and we have confirmed with the DRC that these people, places, and Ages actually exist. We hope that, by sharing them with our readers, we can contribute to a greater understanding of the lost empire of D'ni.

Jill Hinckley

Jill Hinckley, Prima Games

PRIMA GAMES
A Division of Prima Publishing
3000 Lava Ridge Court
Roseville, CA 95661
P 916.787.7000 F 916.787.7004
www.primagames.com

The Cleft

Introduction

It's hard for me to remember the life I led before I started writing this book, and now that I've finished it, there's certainly no way I could go back to being the person I was. The things that I'm about to describe—the things I actually experienced—are so unbelievable that most people who read this book may think I'm either trying to fool them or that I've gone completely around the bend.

I shouldn't let that bother me, but it does. I don't blame anyone who shares that opinion; on the contrary, I understand, believe me. If you had told me a few months ago that just by writing the right words on the right paper with the right ink, you could explore an infinite number of worlds, I would have handed you a dollar and told you not to spend it on booze. But now. . . .

I'm getting ahead of myself. Let me start at the beginning. I used to write video game strategy guides—a good job, but not one known for having a high excitement factor, or even a high leaving-the-house factor. This suited me just fine; the outside world and I have never been on the best of terms.

My involvement with this book began a few weeks ago with an e-mail from an editor for whom I'd worked in the past. She had another project to offer me: some sort of travel journal for a place called "D'ni," and she asked me to call her immediately.

A travel journal? I'd never written a travel journal before. I had no idea how to even begin such a task. I could barely handle sending postcards while on vacation. And besides, I'd much prefer a job that I could do from home. If pressed, I'd have to admit that there was something about the offer that piqued my interest, something I couldn't quite put my finger on. But as curious as I was about the project, I knew I would have to turn it down. What business did someone like me have writing something like that?

After several minutes of trying to figure out how to pronounce "D'ni" ("duh-NEE?" "DIN-nee?"), I made the call to my editor, quickly explained my concerns, and asked her if she really thought I was qualified to take on the project. To my dismay, she'd anticipated that very same question and had a ready answer.

"Did you ever play the PC games *Myst* and *Riven*?" she asked.

"Sure, me and about a billion other people," I replied.

"Well, this D'ni is supposedly where the guys who made those games got their ideas from. There's a group called the D'ni Restoration Council, and they're opening some of the areas of D'ni to a few explorers. We've got exclusive permission to send someone down and write a book about it, and since you're already familiar with the *Myst* games, I think you'd be a good fit."

Now, freelance writers who don't work don't eat, and freelance writers who make a habit of turning down jobs for no good reason don't get offered work in the future. So with my best excuse shot down, I had no choice but to accept.

My editor filled me in on the particulars of the project: I was to travel to an undisclosed location in the middle of a desert somewhere in the southwestern United States, where I'd meet a Dr. Richard Watson of the D'ni Restoration Council (DRC). He would take me to D'ni, which apparently was an underground city deep below the surface and thousands of years old.

I stifled a groan. This sounded like a real *Weekly World News* story. I was amazed my editor was able to assign it to me without busting out laughing. Still, maybe there was an angle to work here: crackpot archaeologists, mad from the desert heat, imagining ancient subterranean cities—if I couldn't get some interesting stories out of that situation, I had no business calling myself a writer.

But there was something else there, too. No matter how many reasons there were to decline the project (and there were plenty), I felt as if I had to accept it. Not for the paycheck or to keep myself in my editor's good graces, or for any solid, logical reason; I just had to see this D'ni for myself. I wouldn't have been able to admit it at the time, but I was drawn to it.

I spent the next week reading through *The Book of Atrus*, *The Book of Ti'ana*, and *The Book of D'ni*, three books of alleged D'ni history sent to me by the DRC that looked and read more like paperback fantasy novels than historical documents. But I decided that if I was going to speak to these DRC nutcases as if I was taking them seriously, I'd better have my facts straight.

The Book of Atrus was the coming-of-age story of Atrus, around whom most of the *Myst* franchise revolved. He was raised in a desert Cleft by his grandmother, Anna, and taken to the city of D'ni by his estranged father, Gehn, during his adolescence. Gehn showed Atrus the art of Writing, which was the D'ni ability to create "links" to pre-existing worlds by using precise language and special Linking Books and ink. Gehn considered himself a god of the worlds he linked to (he claimed that he created them out of nothingness), but he was revealed to be thoroughly mortal by the end of the story. Atrus imprisoned his father in the Riven Age and eloped with a native of Riven, Catherine. Catherine and Atrus' grandmother, Anna, Wrote the Myst Age, and Atrus, Catherine, and Anna retired to it once Gehn was imprisoned.

The Book of Ti'ana was the story of Anna's discovery of the underground city of D'ni ("Ti'ana" was her D'ni name). She was a human woman who found an entrance to the city after the death of her father and was the first contact the D'ni had ever had with anyone from the earth's surface. Throughout the course of the story, she earned the respect of most D'ni and the heart of a D'ni named Aitrus. Unfortunately, she pled for the life of a disgraced and exiled nobleman named Veovis, which indirectly allowed him to return to D'ni and release a plague that destroyed the culture. Though Aitrus died as well, he fathered Gehn before his passing. After the fall of D'ni, Anna returned to the Cleft to live.

The Book of D'ni told the story of the events following the *Riven* game. Atrus and Catherine returned to D'ni and explored the Ages of the D'ni Linking Books to try and find survivors. They also discovered a sealed Linking Book to the Age of Terahnee, which seemed to be a paradise until it was revealed that its splendor was made possible by the brutal exploitation of a race of slaves called the *relyimah*. Terahnee's tyranny came to an end when the ruling class began to die of a sickness that the D'ni had brought with them through the link. After helping the *relyimah* form a new society, Atrus and Catherine linked to a new Age to begin building a new D'ni, and Catherine gave birth to their daughter, Yeesha.

I also took a few days to reacquaint myself with the *Myst* games; I'd forgotten how beautiful and alien the Ages of those games were. Despite my skepticism, I found myself becoming excited about seeing the DRC's version of D'ni, even though I was sure that the "real" D'ni would be a disappointment after seeing its fictional counterpart.

So engrossed in my studies was I that I still don't remember much of the flight that began my journey. I couldn't even say for sure which airport it was that I flew into, nor do I remember the name of the friendly yet slightly manic DRC volunteer who met me at the airport and drove me out into the desert.

As we approached the foot of a dormant volcano, the driver's cell phone rang. He answered and immediately launched into an animated conversation with whoever was on the other end of the line. In the middle of a particularly colorful string of profanity, he skidded to a halt just beyond a gate in the middle of a long barbed-wire fence.

"I've got to go back," he said. "You'll have to walk from here."

"Walk?" I said, grabbing the backpack that contained my notebook, tape recorder, and camera. "Walk where?"

He pointed toward the volcano. "Wait at the Cleft for Dr. Watson." He didn't even wait for me to shut the door before throwing the truck into reverse and roaring back the way we came.

So there I was, stuck in the middle of the desert, with only vague directions from someone who might or might not have belonged to an insane archaeologists' club. I realized then that I didn't even know exactly which state I was in, which did nothing to calm my nerves. Fortunately, the sun was still fairly low in the sky, and a gentle breeze whipped across the desert plain. From what I knew of deserts, they rarely offered much better hiking conditions.

Outside the Cleft

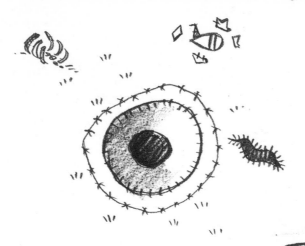

No Trespassing

A less than auspicious beginning.

No trespassing sign. Land owned by Elias Zandi.

A large sign rested against the fence near where my erstwhile driver dropped me off. I approached it and tried to make out the faded letters:

*PRIVATE PROPERTY
NO TRESPASSING*

*Trespassing for any purpose is strictly prohibited.
Violators will be prosecuted.*

Property owner: Elias Zandi

I checked out the back of the sign, where I saw what looked like a scrap of burlap cloth with the image of a hand on it. I reached up to touch it, and as soon as I did, the thumb of the insignia glowed a bright blue for a few seconds.

Strange burlap cloth on back of sign. Touched it, and it glowed.

Startled, I touched it again, just to make sure that the desert heat wasn't making me hallucinate. The same thing happened. Was this some sort of fiber-optic gimmick? If so, what was the point of it? All of a sudden, I had my first questions for Dr. Watson.

Meeting Zandi

Zandi's trailer, to the right of the volcano.

Zandi—strange guy, but harmless. Helpful, even.

With nowhere else to go, I took my driver's advice and started walking toward the volcano. After a few minutes, I saw some sort of structure at its base, which I began to run toward. As I approached, I could see that it was a small camper with a yellow awning, under which a man sat reading a book. Figuring that he must be Dr. Watson, I pulled out my tape recorder and approached. Before I could say anything, he greeted me with the following enigmatic salutation:

Another cloth hanging behind trailer. Touched this one too.

"Hey. Welcome. So, uh, I'm Zandi. I probably know more about why you're here then you do. Don't worry about it. You felt drawn here, just like the others. I'm not really here to give you answers, just to give you help and get you started. She's left a message for you in the Cleft. Listen to it well. Follow her. Find the Journeys and then enter the tree. Oh, and, uh, check with me if you need help."

I guessed that this was the "Zandi" referred to as the property owner on the No Trespassing sign, but Zandi corrected me. He was actually Jeff Zandi, the son of the late Elias Zandi, who owned the property. Slightly unnerved by his apparent lack of familiarity with reality, I walked around behind his camper, where I saw another one of those burlap cloths with the hand prints on them. As before, I touched it, and this time, the thumb and half the palm glowed blue for a few seconds.

I returned to Zandi to ask him what the burlap cloths were, but he wasn't interested in talking about them. "Well," he said, "you're going to need power for that Imager in the Cleft. Try releasing the brake on the windmill first." I saw the windmill near a fence beyond the trailer, but what exactly was this Cleft that he spoke of?

The Cleft

The windmill that Zandi told me to start.

The Cleft, where Atrus and Anna (Ti'ana) supposedly lived.

I decided to investigate the windmill, and that's when I saw the Cleft: a huge rip in the surface of the earth, at least 80 feet long by 20 or 30 feet deep. At one end of the Cleft floor was a pool of water. Rope bridges crisscrossed its levels, leading to rooms that looked as if they were carved out of the Cleft's rock walls. I had seen sketches of this Cleft before in The Book of Atrus. This is where the legendary Atrus from the Myst games was supposed to have been raised by his grandmother, Anna (a.k.a. Ti'ana, the first human woman to see the city of D'ni in their recorded history).

Of course, it wasn't possible that this could be the actual Cleft. I was obviously dealing with some very committed Myst enthusiasts who'd gone to great lengths to replicate the childhood home of one of their favorite fictional characters. Still, it was a good likeness of the Cleft, and I couldn't even begin to imagine how much time and effort it must have taken to create.

Telescope Ruins and Wahrk Skeleton

Ruins of Riven telescope.

Wahrk skeleton. Shark/whale hybrid apparently didn't thrive in desert.

Another Journey Cloth hanging on Wahrk's jawbone.

Reassured by the proximity of the Cleft's shelter and fresh water, I decided to do a bit more exploring before the heat became too intense. After all, Dr. Watson wasn't here yet, and Zandi would surely tell him of my arrival.

I walked past the Cleft, away from Zandi's trailer, where I saw some oddly familiar ruins. It took me a moment to place them, but I almost laughed out loud when I did; they made a perfect replica of the telescope that was sucked into the Star Fissure at the end of <u>Riven</u>! So this is where it wound up, eh? I had to hand it to the DRC; they had really taken obsessive fandom to a new level.

Just beyond the telescope was the skeleton of an enormous beast, seemingly half whale and half shark. Once again, I recalled seeing something like it in <u>Riven</u>; I think they were called "Wahrks." I walked up to the Wahrk skeleton and touched it. To my amazement, whatever the DRC had constructed it from looked and felt exactly like bone.

Hanging inside the Wahrk's jawbone was another one of those burlap cloths. I touched it, and this time, the thumb and entire palm lit up. As I did so, something that Zandi said came back to me: find the Journeys. Was he talking about these cloths? I'd found three of them so far, and the odds were good that I'd find more. For lack of a better term, I decided to call them Journey Cloths.

In the Cleft

Fourth Journey Cloth

Entering the Cleft. Camera's timer seems to work fine.

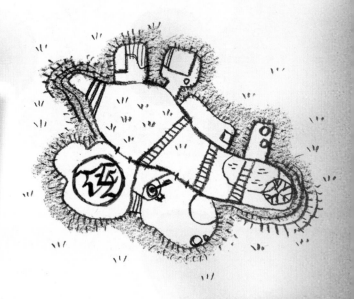

There was nothing else to see outside of the Cleft besides a barbed-wire fence that kept me from climbing to the top of the volcano. That suited me just fine, as the heat was already becoming a bit too intense for my taste. I really didn't feel compelled to mess around near a lava vent.

I returned to the ladder that led into the Cleft and climbed down into it, grateful for the relief from the blazing desert sun. As I stood in the Cleft, I was astounded at the level of detail the DRC had put into it. In fact, against my better judgment, I had gone beyond wondering <u>how</u> the DRC had done it and started wondering <u>if</u> they had done it at all. Obviously, the <u>Myst</u> stories could

This bridge looked more sturdy than it was.

View from the bottom of the Cleft, after bridge snapped.

Broken bridges still make good ladders.

not possibly have been true, but I was finding it harder and harder to believe that this Cleft could possibly be the work of a group of <u>Myst</u> fanatics, no matter how crazed or well funded.

Fourth Journey Cloth at top of bridge "ladder," with handsome guy touching it. Ha ha.

Both possibilities seemed equally impossible, so I put the question out of my mind and decided to poke around the Cleft a bit. Two bridges stretched from the bottom of the ladder. One had a gaping hole in the middle of it and led to a closed door on a narrow ledge, so I decided to cross the other one, which was intact and led to an open door.

Bad decision. As soon as I entrusted my entire body weight to the bridge, it snapped, and I fell to the floor of the Cleft. Fortunately, it happened so suddenly that I didn't even realize what had happened until I'd landed safely on the mossy floor without injury. The floor of the Cleft was covered with small blue flowers, just as described in <u>The Book of Atrus</u>. Once again, I was amazed by the level of detail the Cleft's designers had put into their work.

I walked along the floor away from the pool and found another broken bridge that I could climb like a ladder. It led up to a crude sleeping chamber, just like the one Atrus and Anna supposedly used.

Another of those Journey Cloths hung on the wall. I touched it, and the thumb, palm, and index finger glowed. I'd found four Journey Cloths so far, and each one lit up more of the hand image. There were three unlit "fingers" left; did that mean that I could expect to find three more Journey Cloths?

Atrus' Letter

Next to the sleeping chamber with the Journey Cloth was another sleeping chamber. A letter lay on the bed. I picked it up and read it:

Our dearest Yeesha,

Last night your mother had a dream. We know that some futures are not cast, by writer or Maker, but the dream tells that D'ni will grow again someday. New seekers of D'ni will flow in from the desert, feeling called to something they do not understand.

But the dream also tells of a desert bird with the power to weave this new D'ni's future. We fear such power—it changes people.

Yeesha, our desert bird, your search seems to take you further and further from us. I hope that what you find will bring you closer.

—Your Father, Atrus

I shook my head. I had to give the DRC credit for their attention to detail, but this was just silly. And I didn't even understand the meaning of the handwritten notes in the margins: "I will use them to bring me the Least . . . Impossible . . . Now his burden is mine . . . What I have found must be returned." I placed it back on the bed and decided I'd ask Dr. Watson about that one too when I saw him.

Laboratory

Stepped off of this ledge outside "bedroom" to reach wooden plank bridge.

Planks were solid enough to walk across.

Climbed up another bridge "ladder" on other side of Cleft to reach laboratory.

Exiting the sleeping chamber, I turned right and dropped onto a small ledge at one end of a crude bridge made of three long boards. I walked across the boards to the other side of the Cleft, turned left, and dropped down to another narrow ledge. From here, I could climb up the remains of the bridge that had snapped under me and reach the open doorway.

As I passed through the doorway, I realized that the room beyond it was meant to be the laboratory that Atrus and Anna used at the beginning of _The Book of Atrus_. On the walls of the laboratory hung sketches of the volcanic cap that young Atrus designed to charge up a battery. Several old books, stone samples, and smashed pieces of furniture lay scattered around the laboratory, which had obviously seen better days.

The laboratory.

Button next to door doesn't do anything—no power? Weird symbols next to it.

Close-up on symbols. These are important?

But why would the DRC go to all the trouble of recreating the Cleft in such a ruined state? I knew that the events of _The Book of Atrus_ were supposed to have taken place about 200 years ago, but it seemed to me that die-hard fans of the _Myst_ series would want to recreate the Cleft in its prime, not in this condition.

URU
AGES BEYOND MYST.
Prima's Official Travel Guide

Inside of the entrance was a glowing blue button. As I approached it to push it, I kicked a board out of the way and revealed a pattern that had been etched into the wall. Nothing happened when I pushed the button, but then I recalled Zandi saying that I'd have to release the brake on the windmill if I wanted to restore power in the Cleft.

Device to left of doorway as I entered the laboratory.

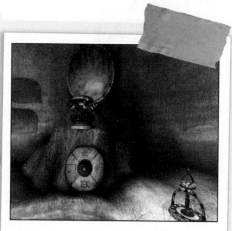

Device opposite doorway.

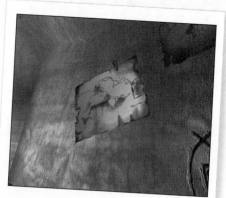

Atrus's sketches, as seen in
Book of Atrus?

Two other devices were in the laboratory: a stone dish on a ledge near the door that had a light in front of it, and a much more elaborate mechanism on the wall opposite the door. Neither seemed to work, but I was curious. I decided to try to restore power to the Cleft so I could figure out exactly what these machines did. And, to be quite honest, I was starting to believe that this might actually be the Cleft that Atrus and Anna had lived in. For my own peace of mind, I needed to see that these devices did nothing remarkable when powered up.

Kitchen

Between the two laboratory machines was a doorway leading into a crude kitchen. The door in the far wall was closed and locked, and a blue stone glowed dully next to it. Like its counterpart in the laboratory, the blue stone did nothing when I pushed it—no power.

Stone table for food preparation?

Windmill shaft and brake lever, I think.

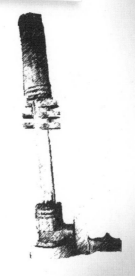

A large lever stood out from the ground near the laboratory doorway, and a huge shaft ran from the base of the lever up into the ceiling. After a few seconds of calculating the spatial relations, I realized that the shaft led up to the windmill on the surface. The lever must be the windmill brake. I pulled the lever, and the windmill brake released, but the windmill didn't start turning. I decided to head up to the surface to investigate further.

Starting the Windmill

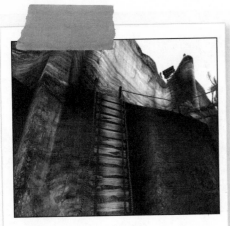

It wasn't a good bridge, but it made a good ladder.

Pushed this lever to get windmill turning, which restored power.

To leave the Cleft, I simply walked out of the laboratory and dropped to the floor of the Cleft. I then walked over to the remains of the bridge that had snapped under me and climbed it to reach the ladder that led to the surface.

Because Zandi told me about the windmill in the first place, I asked him if he had any advice. "Sometimes the windmill seizes up," he said. "Try starting it by hand."

I approached the windmill and found that I could push a long handle on its base to get it going. After half of a rotation's worth of pushing, the windmill started turning of its own accord. Lucky I chose a breezy day to visit.

Laboratory Devices: Door and Hologram Page

I went back to Zandi to tell him that I got the windmill working, but he seemed vaguely annoyed. "Listen," he said, "you're still missing the message she's left in the Imager. Make sure you see that before you enter the tree."

Pushing this button opened and closed the door.

Some kind of hologram of a piece of paper? Didn't do much.

At this point, I didn't know who was crazier: Zandi for giving me these ridiculous hints, or me for taking his advice. Still, now that the Cleft's power was restored, I resolved to debunk the DRC by closely examining the toys they'd created. Zandi gave me another hint: "All right, for the Imager, there are symbols next to the door. You've got to enter those to get her message."

I headed back into the Cleft and climbed across the ledges and fragments of bridges just as before to reach the laboratory again. Now that power was restored, the lights on the two devices glowed brightly, as did the button on the inside of the door.

I pressed the button next to the door, and it slammed shut; pretty clever, but certainly not beyond the limits of everyday human ingenuity. I did, however, make a note of the symbols next to the door, which Zandi seemed to think were so important.

The mechanism next to the door, with its green light, was a bit more impressive. I pressed the green button, and something flashed in front of my face for half a second before fading out. I pressed the button a few more times to get a better look at it; it seemed to be a crude hologram of a page from a book. This was more impressive than the door mechanism, but it still wasn't proof of an advanced ancient culture.

Activating the Imager

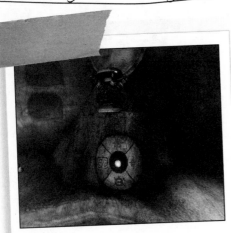

Imager was powered on after windmill started turning.

Matched symbols to the ones etched into the wall near door.

The machine that Zandi referred to as an Imager was another story. I touched the blue button on its front to activate it. Just as Zandi had said, four symbols were at the front of it, similar to those next to the laboratory door. It looked just like a puzzle from one of the <u>Myst</u> games.

I guessed that I had to change the symbols on the Imager to match the ones next to the door, but I didn't see any way to do it. While investigating the Imager, I touched one of the incorrect symbols and was astonished to see it fade away, only to be replaced by another symbol. I was so shocked that I didn't even try to figure out how such a thing was possible; I just changed the symbols so that they matched the ones etched into the wall near the door. Nothing happened.

Hologram of woman?! That technology doesn't exist!

I'd almost given up the Imager as a hoax when I pressed the blue button in the center of the symbols. Suddenly, a grainy hologram of a woman appeared and started to speak! As a reflex, I turned on my tape recorder to capture the words that I could hardly believe I was hearing:

"Sho-rah. Re-koo-ahn tre-Cleft pre-niv le-glo-en b'rem. Oh yes, not in D'ni, they won't understand.

"Once again the stream in the Cleft has begun to flow. It was dry for so long. The water is flowing in from the desert. The storm is coming."

The translucent woman stood in the laboratory doorway that I'd closed only a couple of minutes ago. I realized that she would have been staring at the pool at the bottom of the Cleft, had the door been open. She then traced her finger over the symbols next to the door, the ones I had entered into the Imager.

"Have you heard of the city," she continued, "the deep city—the ancient Uru—where there was power to write worlds? For thousands of years the city lived—lived beneath the surface—keeper of the secret, keeper of the power, keeper of the ages. Always keeping.

URU

AGES BEYOND MYST.

Prima's Official Travel Guide

"The city grew proud. And then it died."

The image of the woman danced a lilting waltz to the other side of the laboratory. It reminded me of something I read in <u>The Book of Atrus</u>, how Anna would dance when an infrequent rainstorm came to the desert. The vision of the woman continued speaking as she danced:

"The water flows where it wills. It seeks its own path, uncontrolled. Except that it flows downward, always downward.

"D'ni, the city of ages, of other worlds, died. But now it breathes again, it awaits.

"Some will seek that destination. But you should seek the journey. It's as a fine tapestry, complex beyond comprehension, but now torn."

With a wave of her hand, she revealed a Journey Cloth on the wall next to the Imager.

She revealed the fifth Journey Cloth on the wall of the lab.

Didn't see any projectors. Could put my hand right through her.

"We will show you remnants, pieces of the tapestry, pieces of the Journey. Find these remnants, these Journeys—seven. Seven in each Age. Seven here in the desert. Consider it a quest. No—a request. Worship.

-26-

"The water flows downward. And there
it pools and collects and finally, once again, it reaches the roots. And the tree
begins to grow again.

"I am Yeesha. My parents brought me to this place.

"We will bring you."

Yeesha's Words

The image of Yeesha flickered out of existence, and I was left with nothing but the
sound of the windmill's slow grinding for company. Numbed with disbelief, I
pressed the blue button on the Imager again, and again the image of Yeesha acted
out her recorded message. As she did, I looked in every corner of the laboratory for
hidden projectors. I put my hand through the image and felt nothing. The technology
was far beyond what human science was capable of. There was no rational explanation for it—unless the stories were true. Unless D'ni actually existed.

But if that were true, what was Yeesha trying to say? There was no "stream in
the Cleft" or "water flowing in from the desert." And in my <u>Myst</u> research, I
hadn't come across a city named "Uru," nor any city that had been destroyed out of
pride. Was this another name for the city of D'ni, which was destroyed by the
traitorous actions of a few of its corrupt citizens? Yeesha also seemed to draw a
distinction between those who would seek the "destination" (D'ni itself) and the
"journey," apparently favoring the latter.

Yeesha was the daughter of Atrus and his wife, Catherine; that much I
remembered from <u>The Book of D'ni</u>. But Atrus and Catherine didn't have the best
luck with their kids. Their sons were Sirrus and Achenar, the brothers from the
original <u>Myst</u> game, who abused the D'ni art of using Linking Books by enslaving
the people of those worlds. For their crimes, Atrus imprisoned them in Prison
Books. I remember thinking it odd that Atrus and Catherine, who seemed to be
fundamentally decent people, would produce such rotten offspring. Maybe Yeesha

was the one they got right. After all, Yeesha spoke of a proud city being destroyed by its own pride, which didn't sound like her brothers at all; they were more like their grandfather, Gehn, who saw himself as a god in the Ages he linked to.

I realized then that I had a decision to make. I could either wait near the Cleft for Dr. Watson to show up and have the DRC bring me to D'ni. Or, if Yeesha actually existed, I could undertake the journey she spoke of so highly. I can't say for sure that I was absolutely convinced of the existence of D'ni and its people at this point, but I couldn't come up with any more plausible explanation for what I'd seen so far. And Yeesha, whether she was real or a figment of someone's imagination, had my undivided attention.

Fifth Journey Cloth

Not knowing what else to do, I touched the Journey Cloth that Yeesha's image revealed during her speech. The thumb, palm, and first two fingers lit up. This was the fifth Journey Cloth I'd touched in the Cleft and surrounding area. Yeesha said that there were seven Journeys in each Age, including the desert. That meant that I only had two left to find.

Journey Cloth #5. Two more to go?

At this point, I decided to retrace my steps. I'd taken a few pictures so far, but I decided to make sure I'd photographed everything that I had done and make notes in the margins of the photos. That way, I could use those notes to remind myself of exactly what I'd seen and write full journal entries later. Fortunately, I'd brought plenty of film, and my camera had a built-in timer, so I could even set up shots with me in them to prove that I'd actually experienced the unbelievable events I'd photographed.

Above all, I wanted to make sure that the story of the Cleft got out, even if something happened to me and I wasn't able to tell it. Although writers don't generally like to admit it, I knew that each picture I took would be worth a thousand words. And while most people would dismiss my experiences as a hoax no matter how carefully I tried to document them, the photos would make it that much harder to do so. Above all, I hoped that someone out there would be able to suspend their disbelief and feel the call, as I had.

Sixth Journey Cloth

Bridge leading from kitchen. Had to jump gap in the middle of it.

Sixth J.C. on back of closed lab door!

Six down, one to go.

I left the door to the laboratory closed, because the bridge that led to it was broken and useless. Instead, I walked through the kitchen and pressed the blue button next to its closed door, which slid open.

The bridge beyond the door led to the entrance of the Cleft, but it was missing a couple of planks. Placing a foot on the bridge, I gradually leaned onto it until I was sure that it would hold my weight. I carefully approached the gap in the bridge and hopped across it to reach the other side of the Cleft.

I turned around to look back at the doorways to the laboratory and kitchen. To my surprise, there was a Journey Cloth on the back of the closed laboratory door! For a third time, I retraced my steps up to the ledge in front of the laboratory door and placed my hand on the Journey Cloth. Six down, one to go.

Pool and Tree

Water in the pool was surprisingly fresh.

Door in tree. Wouldn't open when I touched it.

Hard to see, but J.C. #7 was on side of bucket.

So far, I hadn't really explored the other half of the Cleft floor, which held the small pool of water and a huge tree. The water in the pool was fresh and cool to the touch, and at the base of the tree was a door marked with the same hand symbol that I'd seen on the Journey Cloths.

I approached the door and placed my hand on the symbol, figuring that this must be the seventh Journey Cloth, but nothing happened. It was then that I remembered Zandi's first words of advice: "Find the Journeys, and then enter the tree." Maybe this door would open once I found the seventh Journey Cloth?

I sat on a rock near the edge of the pool to collect my thoughts. Where could that seventh Journey Cloth be? As my eyes wandered around the Cleft, I caught sight of a bucket overhead—and it had the seventh Journey Cloth on the side of it!

Seventh Journey Cloth and Opening the Tree

Crossed another dodgy bridge to reach ledge w/ bucket.

Stepping on footbrake lowered bucket to the Cleft floor.

I climbed up the Cleft wall to another dilapidated bridge. I crossed the bridge, hopping across a gap in the planks, to reach a narrow ledge near the bucket. A small pantry had been hollowed out of the Cleft wall at the end of the bridge, but nothing of interest was inside—just a few earthenware pots that looked as if they hadn't been used in centuries.

Touched door after getting all
7 J.C.'s, and door opened!

Jumped down to Cleft floor and
touched seventh Journey Cloth.

Of much greater interest to me was the pulley mechanism for the Journey Cloth bucket at the end of the ledge I stood on. I tried to stretch my arm around the side of the bucket to touch the Journey Cloth, but I couldn't quite reach it. By sheer chance, I accidentally stepped on the mechanism's foot brake, which lowered the bucket to the floor of the Cleft.

Without wasting a second, I dropped from the ledge into the pool below. I scrambled over to the bucket and touched the Journey Cloth. The entire hand image lit up, indicating that I'd found all seven desert Journey Cloths.

And now, it was time for the moment of truth. I walked over to the door at the base of the tree and touched the hand symbol. It glowed for a few seconds, just as the last Journey Cloth had, and then the door slid into the floor of the Cleft, revealing a ladder that led down into a hidden passage in the Cleft floor.

The C'left Cavern

Don't know what this rune
meant. D'ni writing in center?

That's me. That's a Linking
Book?! Undoctored photo,
I swear!

I climbed down the ladder and into a narrow cavern that ran
under the Cleft. As I stepped off the ladder, a large round blue
sigil began glowing on the cavern wall. I couldn't
make any sense of the designs that lined its
perimeter, but the symbols in the center seemed to
be D'ni writing, from what I remembered of it
from the <u>Myst</u> games and novels. The symbol's
glow faded as I stepped away from it.

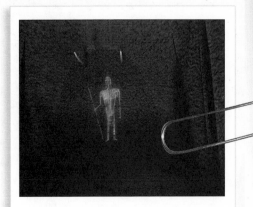

The cavern opened into a small room with a
short path that led up to a book on a pedestal.
My heart rose into my throat as I approached
it. If the stories were true, and if D'ni really
existed, could this be . . . a Linking Book? If I

Human (D'ni?) holding
stick or pole.

touched it, would I actually be transported to another world—another Age—via a
mystical link that had been written into existence by a D'ni scholar?

Before I touched the Linking Book, I looked around at the five blue sigils etched into the rock walls of the small room. I studied their shapes and pondered their meanings as their blue glow pulsed slowly in the dimly lit cavern.

The first sigil, on the wall to the right of the cavern as I entered, appeared to be a bipedal humanoid figure holding a staff or pole in its right hand. Looking from right to left around the room, I saw sigils in the shape of a counterclockwise spiral (like the one in the center of the Journey Cloth palm symbol), a book with a D'ni symbol on it, a city in a cavern (D'ni?), and a volcano under a night sky, which might have been meant to represent the very volcano that stood

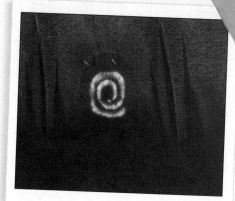

Spiral, like the palm of the hand symbol.

Linking Book, I think

City of D'ni? Definitely city; think it's in a cavern.

outside the Cleft. These sigils obviously held some sort of significance, but aside from their superficial meanings, I couldn't even begin to decipher them; I didn't even know if I was supposed to read them from right to left, or left to right.

Only one other item of significance was in the room: the Book. I approached it and took a closer look. Sure enough, it seemed to be a Linking Book. A panel on the right page showed the image of a misty island, and beneath it was the same D'ni sigil I saw when I first entered the cavern.

Taking a deep breath, I picked up the Book. I noticed a clip on the back of it that seemed to be intended to attach it to the user's belt, so I clipped the Linking Book to my hip, opened the Book to its linking panel, and placed my palm on the linking panel.

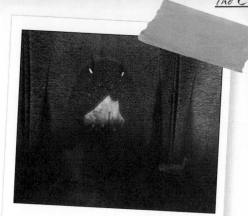

Looks like volcano near Cleft.

Looks like a Linking Book.

Here goes nothing.

At once, I felt the peculiar sensation of linking described so many times in the _Myst_ novels: It was as if I was shrinking and the Linking Book was expanding, pulling me into the fibers of the page.

Oh my God, I thought. _It's all true._

Everything faded to black.

Relto

EDITOR'S NOTE:
Unlike the other chapters in the author's journal, which were
written in a very linear fashion, this chapter was a jumble of
crossed-out and inserted paragraphs, implying that parts of it
were written at different times. Some pages were torn out of the
original journal and other loose pages were inserted at various
points. We have made our best attempt to present this chapter in
the form in which we believe the author intended it to be read.

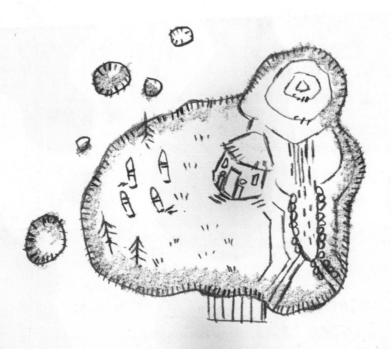

Hut

Pedestals

The walls of the Cleft cavern faded away and were replaced with the eerie mists of the island Age that I would later come to know as Relto. When I first arrived, Relto seemed to be nothing more than a tiny island with a small hut and four pedestals. However, throughout the course of my journey through the Ages, I would return to Relto many times and realize that, although small, this "hub" Age was vitally important to my quest.

I began by exploring the island. It didn't take long. The aforementioned hut and pedestals were at opposite ends of it, and I could see the entire island from just about any point on it. The terrain was much like that of the desert around the Cleft, although a handful of small shrubs stubbornly managed to eke out an existence from the arid, rocky soil.

A thick, impenetrable fog surrounded the entire island. It was impossible to tell how high up I was or if there was anything else on the horizon other than miles and miles of mist. Although the sky was light, I couldn't see a sun (if, in fact, that's what illuminated the sky in this Age). I was simultaneously thrilled to experience my first link to another Age and uneasy to have landed in such a hostile environment.

Suddenly, it dawned on me that I had no way to link back to the Cleft, to Earth! The Linking Book that I picked up in the cavern of the Cleft transported me to Relto, but I saw no Linking Book on Relto that would bring me back. In a panic, I opened the Linking Book on my hip and slapped my hand against the linking panel.

I linked and reappeared inside the hut on Relto, which struck me as odd. I remembered from my reading that one of the fundamental D'ni linking rules was that one could never link from one location in an Age to another location in the same Age. It wasn't just forbidden, it was considered impossible by every D'ni writer that I'd read about. And yet, here I was, still on Relto. How was that possible?

It was then that I realized another apparent impossibility in Yeesha's Linking Book. When I linked to Relto from the Cleft, the Linking Book came with me. That shouldn't have happened. Linking Books were supposed to stay in the Age from which one linked, not come through the link with the user. As far as I knew, this also was completely unheard of.

In one sense, these "impossibilities" were a great comfort to me, because I realized that if I was in mortal danger in any Age—including Relto—I could quickly "panic link" to safety with the Book on my hip. But I was also apprehensive about Yeesha's unbelievable abilities, which seemed to surpass those of hundreds of generations of D'ni scholars.

Pedestals

There were no convenient answers to my questions, and because I seemed to be stuck on Relto for the time being, I decided to explore its features a bit more.

The four pedestals at the end of the island drew my attention. Each had the familiar hand icon, and when I touched the icon, the bottom

Touching the hand icon revealed a Linking Book in each pedestal.

of the pedestal opened to reveal a Linking Book. Before I used any of the Books to link to another Age, however, I wanted to explore this one more thoroughly.

Prima's Official Travel Guide

Other Pedestal Features

At this point, I would like to mention a few other features of the pedestals that I wouldn't discover until later in my journey. I mention them now just for the sake of keeping all of the relevant Relto information in one place in this journal.

I would discover later that once I used a pedestal's Linking Book, that Book disappeared from the pedestal and reappeared in my Library in the hut, where I could use it to link to its Age as many times as I wanted.

Furthermore, after I linked to an Age, I found that I could return to Relto and touch the hand icon on the Age's respective pedestal to see how many Journey Cloths I'd found in that Age so far. Yeesha had told me that there would be seven Journey Cloths in each Age, and she was correct.

Finally, I also discovered that when I found and took a Bahro Pillar from the Bahro Cave at the end of an Age's quest, the Bahro Pillar appeared atop its respective pedestal in Relto.

This information might seem a bit confusing now, but I can tell you from experience that I wish I had known it when I first arrived on Relto.

Hut

The small hut at the opposite end of the island from the pedestals was little more than a hexagonal structure with a stone floor, walls, and a straw roof in need of repair. In some ways, it reminded me of Atrus's hut on Myst Island, though much more crude.

On either side of the hut were bookshelves. I would find out later that the empty shelf to the left (as I stood in the doorway, facing in) would be my Library. The Linking Books that I found in the pedestals outside would appear here after I used each for the first time.

It ain't the Ritz, but it's shelter.

Left bookshelf—Library,
where pedestal Linking Books
wound up.

Linking Books

Later on in my journey, once my Library started to fill with Linking Books, I found that by clicking on the tab above the spine of a Linking Book, I could open the Book and use it to link.

I could either touch the linking panel to go to the original link-in point of the Age, or I could touch the Journey Cloth bookmark on the page before the linking panel to link to the last Journey Cloth I touched.

By clicking on the tab below the spine of a Book, I could destroy it and that "instance" of the Age. If I wanted to begin exploring the Age again, I'd have to take the Linking Book from its pedestal again.

Essentially, destroying an instance of an Age would undo all of the changes I had made to it, and when I linked back to it from its pedestal book, it would be as if I were linking to it for the first time, although the Journey Cloth bookmark would remain intact.

Again, these concepts might seem confusing at the moment, but for the sake of my own obsessive-compulsive personality, I wanted to make sure that all information relevant to Relto appeared in this chapter.

The right bookshelf contained only one book, which had the same sigil inscribed on its cover that I had seen in the Cleft cavern and in Yeesha's Linking Book. I noticed that the same symbol appeared over both bookshelves in the hut as well. Was this Yeesha's D'ni name? I didn't think that it was a simple coincidence that I kept seeing it as I progressed along the journey that she'd asked me to undertake.

Right bookshelf—
non-linking books

The solitary book on the right bookshelf contained only four pages of writing, each of which was preceded by a design that incorporated a sketch of a pedestal. At first I thought the four designs were identical, but then I realized that each was a subtle variation on the same theme. At the bottom of each page was a single D'ni character, which I assumed were page numbers (1-8). I made a note of them; at least that way, I'd be able to do some rudimentary translation, if the need arose.

After studying the pages of the book for a bit, I realized that each design referred to the page of writing that followed it, and that each page of writing referred to one of the four Ages that the Linking Books in the pedestals linked to. In fact, the design on the top of each pedestal corresponded to one of the designs in the book. Using these clues, I was able to figure out the names of the Ages that the pedestal Books linked to.

PAGES 1 AND 2

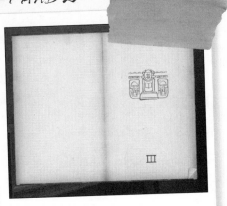

Page design

Pedestal

<u>Age:</u> *Teledahn*

<u>Design Variation:</u> *A cluster of mushrooms.*

<u>Pedestal:</u> *Near right (from hut entrance, facing pedestals)*

<u>Text:</u> *"The truth of a man is found in the darkness beneath the surface. Some light might reveal only what some men want to be seen."*

—Sayings of Regeltavok Oorpah, Book 9, Entry 221, Item 29.

PAGES 3 AND 4

Page design

Pedestal

Age: Gahreesen

Design Variation: Steepled mountains or buildings with eyes.

Pedestal: Far left (from hut entrance, facing pedestals)

Text: "The laws contrived by the proud are their security and their undoing. Such laws make disobedience a virtue and obedience a sin."

—Sayings of Regeltavok Oorpah, Book 12, Entry 32, Item 134.

PAGES 5 AND 6

Page design

Pedestal

Age: Kadish Tolesa

Design Variation: Abstract geometric shapes, possibly a tree or tower?

Pedestal: Far right (from hut entrance, facing pedestals)

Text: "Only the way a man is when he is hidden is how he is. A shallow glimpse can deceive. Look deep, ponder and recognize all that is hidden."

—Sayings of Regeltavok Oorpah, Book 9, Entry 221, Item 77.

Page design

Pedestal

Age: Eder Kemo and Eder Gira

Design Variation: A lake (?) with fish in it.

Pedestal: Near left (from hut entrance, facing pedestals)

Text: "When all is taken from one, the only hope that remains is what is given by another. Through this giving, both are redeemed."

—Sayings of Regeltavok Oorpah, Book 2, Entry 1071, Item 54.

Closet

Another item of note in the hut was the large closet that sat between the two bookshelves, directly opposite the door. When I opened it, I found it filled with

an impossibly huge variety of clothing, all of which fit me perfectly. I might be lost in another world, but at least I wouldn't have to worry about having clean underwear!

The only other item of note in the hut was a mechanism, next to the library bookshelf, that opened and closed the rickety window shades.

Window shade lever

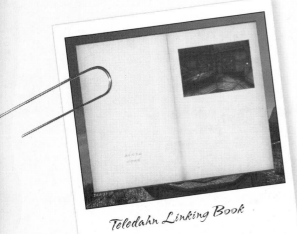

Teledahn Linking Book

After seeing all that there was to see of Relto for the time being, I decided that I might as well link to one of the four Ages provided to me in the pedestal Linking Books. There didn't seem to be any particular limitation on which Age I should visit first, so I decided to link to them in the order they were described in the book I found in the hut: Teledahn first, followed by Gahreesen, Kadish Tolesa, and finally Eder Kemo and Eder Gira.

From the entrance to the hut, I approached the near pillar on the right side of the island and pressed the hand symbol to reveal the Linking Book. Picking up the Book, I laid my hand on the linking panel and felt Relto dissolve around me as I linked to Teledahn.

Yeesha Pages

Later in my journey, I would find sheets of paper that, for lack of a better term, I decided to call Yeesha Pages. These Pages fit perfectly into Yeesha's Linking Book, and I found that when I linked back to Relto with them in my Book, they added new features to the Age.

Furthermore, by opening Yeesha's Linking Book and flipping through the Pages, I found that I could enable and disable the Yeesha Page effects by laying my hand on the Yeesha Pages. The writing on an active Yeesha Page glowed brightly, and the writing on a deactivated Yeesha Page did not.

Each Age contained at least one Yeesha Page. The following chapters describe exactly where I found each Page, so I won't go into detail about that now.

EDITOR'S NOTE:
The author makes reference to receiving one additional Yeesha Page at his journey's end, in addition to the ones shown below. However, he made it quite clear in his manuscript that he did not want any information regarding the final Page revealed until the end of his narrative. Therefore, in accordance with the author's wishes, the details of this final Page are described at the end of the chapter entitled "Return to the Cleft."

Hut Roof—Teledahn, next to office fish tank

URU
AGES BEYOND MYST.
Prima's Official Travel Guide

Sticks and Stones—Gahreesen, inside crevasse near KI Dispenser

Tree—Kadish, near waterfront after glowing symbol path

Waterfall—Gahreesen, in a prison cell

Rug—Eder Kemo, on a ledge near the "brain trees"

Teledahn

Arriving in Teledahn
The Cabin and First Journey Cloth

My link-in point: a wooden cabin.

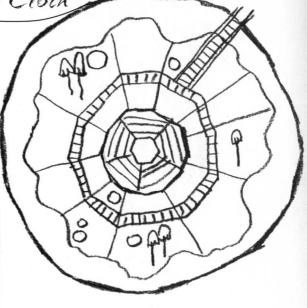

Locked grate in the floor. Water below it.

The first Journey Cloth, on the back of the cabin.

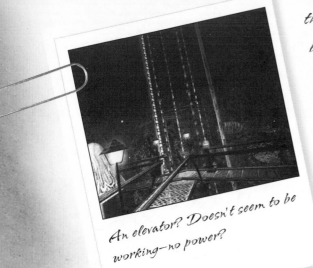

An elevator? Doesn't seem to be working—no power?

My link to Teledahn caused me to appear inside a small hexagonal wooden cabin. In the center of the floor was a metal grate, but when I tried to open it, I found that it was locked. I did notice water underneath it, however, so it probably wouldn't have done me much good even if I could open it. Aside from some crudely fashioned furniture and tools, nothing of interest was in the cabin.

From the doorway, I could see a metal walkway extending past a giant mushroom. I was surprised to see what I thought were snowflakes falling from the sky, though when I left the cabin to get a closer look, I realized that the "snow" was actually clouds of fungal spores. Not as Christmassy as I'd initially thought.

The wooden cabin, surrounded by giant mushrooms, sat in the middle of a giant water-filled mushroom. While walking around the cabin to get a closer look at the unusual fungi, I saw Teledahn's first Journey Cloth hanging on the back of the cabin and made sure to touch it before continuing.

The cabin was surrounded by two concentric walkways, joined by a small pathway that extended from the doorway of the cabin. At the end of that small pathway was an elaborate pulley mechanism that extended above and beyond the walkway—an elevator, perhaps? I pressed a blue button in front of the mechanism, but nothing happened.

Outside the Mushroom

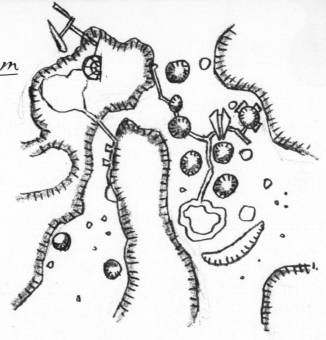

Definitely not in Kansas anymore.

What the heck is that thing? A big bug? A bug-bird?

I followed the outer walkway in a counterclockwise direction from the elevator until I came to another pathway leading out through a crack in the cavern wall.

The sights that greeted me outside of the cavern nearly took my breath away, as did the overpowering aroma of giant fungi growing out of a fetid swamp. I thought that the mushrooms in the cavern were huge, but here I saw mushrooms as large as small skyscrapers! When I turned around, I realized that the "cavern" I'd appeared in was in fact an enormous mushroom itself. Bizarre flying creatures, seemingly half-bird, half-insect, flapped around through the air, and other creatures (or plants?) shaped like lily pads jumped up and down on the surface of the swamp.

The most unusual feature of Teledahn, however, was the sun, which raced around the horizon in a full 360-degree circle once every 65 seconds, neither rising nor setting as it did but remaining at a constant level in the sky. Relto had been strange, but Teledahn was clearly not part of any world that I'd ever seen before.

The Power Tower

Took a left at the first junction in the walkway.

Priming pump. Press three times to raise power tower.

Periscope. Use to move power tower's dish.

I followed the metal walkway until I came to a Y-shaped junction. The right path curved around a huge rock in the distance and disappeared from sight, but the left path led up to a mechanism with two huge camshafts stretching out from it. That seemed to be the more interesting choice, so I walked to the end of the left path.

The path ended in a circular walkway that surrounded two devices: a short cylindrical object with a handle on each side and a taller mechanism that looked like a periscope. I couldn't see anything through the periscope, so I decided to check out its stubbier companion.

The handles on the shorter device didn't seem to move. I pressed down on the top of the device experimentally and heard a sucking sound as the handles rose slightly. It seemed to be some sort of a priming pump.

I pushed down on the top of the pump two more times, and to my surprise, a tower shot up from the center of the platform and extended something that looked like a satellite dish from its top. Once the tower was raised, pulling down on the pump handles collapsed the tower.

While the tower was fully extended, I returned to the periscope to look through it. This time, the viewer was fully operational, and I could look through it to see a craggy rock in the distance.

The power tower when raised.

Used the buttons to move the viewfinder.

After a bit of examination, I discovered that four buttons controlled the viewfinder. The buttons on the right and left sides of the viewer moved it in a clockwise or counterclockwise direction. At the bottom of the viewer were two more buttons that moved it up or down. Pressing a button once caused the viewer to move in that direction until I stopped it by pressing the button that moved it in the opposite direction. I also found that I could cause the viewer to move more quickly by pressing the same button twice.

I used the viewer to look at the surrounding area for a bit, but I felt as if I was missing the point of the mechanism. Because the periscope didn't work until I'd raised the dish tower, I guessed that the periscope controlled the rotation of the dish.

And then there were those camshafts extending out from the base of the platform that I was standing on. Each had a lever in front of it, but pulling the levers didn't activate the shafts; it seemed as if they didn't have any power going to them. Could this entire platform be some sort of power station? If so, how was I supposed to turn it on?

I hated these D'ni puzzles. I could never get through the <u>Myst</u> games without the hint books, but if I didn't figure out the answer to this one, I'd be stuck in Teledahn for a long time. And, to top it off, that crazy circling sun was really starting to drive me nuts.

When the power tower rotated in synch with sun, power was restored.

The sun! Could that be the key? Maybe I was supposed to rotate the tower so that the sun was lined up in the center of the viewer.

Maybe the dish at the top of it was some sort of solar collector.

I put my hypothesis to the test; first, I raised the viewfinder vertically to the level of the sun, and then I pressed the left button to start it rotating counterclockwise. Once the sun reached the center of the viewfinder, I pressed the left button again to match the rotation of the viewfinder to the rotation of the sun, and it worked! A few minutes earlier, the loudest sound I'd heard on Teledahn was the chirping of unseen insects, but now the roar of ancient mechanisms echoed across the surface of the swamp.

Two out of three levers started camshafts rotating after power was restored.

Now it was time to give those camshaft levers a pull. One of them seemed to be broken, but the other two caused the shafts in front of them to start turning. That must have had some effect on the Age.

The Bucket Loader

Left power tower platform and took my first left.

A bucket loader at the end of the pathway.

I left the power tower platform and took a left at the Y-shaped junction, because that was the only pathway I hadn't explored yet. Passing under the nonfunctioning camshaft, I saw that the path ended at what I eventually realized was a bucket-loading mechanism.

A traffic sawhorse? Who left this here? DRC?

Pulling this handle started and stopped buckets.

At the broken end of the pathway was the most unusual thing I'd seen in Teledahn so far: a traffic sawhorse, presumably placed there for safety's sake! This had obviously been brought here from Earth by a fellow human explorer, probably the DRC. It certainly wasn't D'ni, and it didn't seem to be Yeesha's style. Seeing it there, sticking out like a sore thumb, only underscored just how alien Teledahn was to me. And while it was comforting to know that another human being had been here recently, I was also slightly annoyed at how Teledahn's natural landscape had been so callously affected by human hands.

After a bit of trial and error, I figured out how to operate the bucket loader. Pulling the lever in front of it caused the mechanism to start up after about 10 seconds. The buckets were pulled along a cable on giant pulleys, all the way up to the top of the mushroom that I'd linked into.

Pulling the lever again when the loader was activated caused it to gradually slow to a halt, but it was very difficult to get the bucket to stop exactly where I wanted it to stop. The timing was tricky; I had to pull the lever before the bucket was in position, trying to gauge how long it would take for the bucket to grind to a halt.

Riding the Buckets

Ride was freaky, like rundown carnival attraction (how'd I get this picture?)

Pulled the lever and walked quickly but carefully to bucket; was a little tricky getting in!

Looking at the buckets gave me an idea. They were easily large enough to transport a person, although I wasn't sure that was their original purpose. If the pulley mechanism was strong enough, maybe I could activate it, jump quickly into the bucket, and ride to the top of the mushroom. Of course, if it wasn't strong enough, I'd fall into the swamp below.

Bucket dropped me in control room. Definitely meant for cargo, not people.

But, thanks to Yeesha's Linking Book at my side, I could just link back to Relto and get a dry set of clothes from the hut closet. I decided to try it.

It took me a couple of attempts to pull the lever and make it into the bucket before it started to leave. I found that moving carefully and precisely was much more helpful than making a mad, haphazard dash for the bucket.

The bucket ride nearly took my breath away. I didn't have the guts to poke my head out of the top of the bucket, but I could feel myself rising higher and higher into the air. I saw the sky above me replaced by the roof of the cavernous mushroom as the bucket entered its confines, and I prepared to leap out of the bucket.

I shouldn't have bothered. Somehow sensing that the bucket was not empty, the mechanism stopped the bucket over a giant fan in the landing area, and the bottom of the bucket opened, dumping me unceremoniously onto the floor in a cloud of spores. The fan switched on and sucked the spores away, and the bucket resumed its journey in an endless loop.

The Control Room

Second Journey Cloth

Two telescopes in the windows.
No practical purpose.

Second Journey Cloth hung
between the two telescopes.

With Linking Book in Relto, I
could link directly back to last
Journey Cloth I touched, if I
had to leave Teledahn.

So there I was, in a room in the upper part of
the mushroom that I linked into when I first
arrived in Teledahn. The cable and pulley
mechanism continued to move buckets into and
out of the room in an endless cycle.

On one side of the room were two windows
with telescopes in them that overlooked the areas
I'd just explored on foot. Between the two
telescopes was the second Journey Cloth of the
Age, which I made sure to touch. I would now
be able to link directly into this room if I wished, simply by touching the
Journey Cloth bookmark in the Teledahn Linking Book in Relto.
That would save me from having to take another ride in the bucket, which
suited me just fine.

Control Panel

On the opposite side of the room was a control panel and an elevator. I sat down at the control panel to see if I could figure out what exactly it controlled.

In the center of the top part of the panel were four icons. Each of the bottom three icons looked as if it had a drill bit going through it. Lines from all three icons linked them to an icon above them, which looked to have three drill bits coming out of it. These seemed to represent the power tower and the three different camshafts, only two of which worked.

Control panel controls, clockwise from large handle on left: Move buckets, power status lights, light switches, cabin grate lock, open water drain, stop/start buckets.

Below these icons, on the left side of the panel, was a toggle switch that pointed to a round symbol made up of two curved arrows. I flipped the switch down so that it was pointed at a single curved arrow, and the buckets stopped moving after the next bucket entered the control room.

At the far left side of the console was a lever that advanced the buckets one at a time after I'd stopped them. This lever, along with the previous switch, seemed to be intended to give the bucket operator greater control over the conveyor belt, starting and stopping the movement of the buckets at will. That was probably very handy for the bucket operator, but I couldn't figure out how it would help me.

In the middle of the bottom part of the console was another lever. I pulled it and heard water draining from somewhere beneath me. I remembered the water underneath the grate in the cabin that I linked into, which was directly below this control room; could I have just drained it?

To the right of the water lever was another toggle switch with two hexagonal icons. Its current setting showed three bolts penetrating the sides of the hexagon. I flicked the switch so that it pointed to the other icon, which showed the three bolts removed from the hexagon. The metal hatch in the cabin below me was hexagonal—was this the unlocking mechanism?

The only other controls on the panel were three buttons on the right side. Each turned on a set of lights in the control room when I pressed it. Aside from lighting up the dusty room, they didn't seem to serve any purpose.

Elevator

The last item of note in the control room was the elevator. A glowing blue button stood on a pedestal in front of it. I remembered seeing one on the catwalk outside of the cabin downstairs and figured that it must be some sort of a call button. Because the elevator was already on this floor, however, it did nothing when I pushed it.

The elevator. Near blue button was call button. Brown button was "down," blue was "up."

In front of the elevator, near the call button, was a foot pedal that looked as if it was attached to some sort of catch on the base of the elevator. I stepped on it to release the catch, realizing that the elevator probably wouldn't have gone anywhere if I hadn't.

Inside the elevator itself were two more buttons: a blue and a brown. I decided to press the blue one, and the elevator ascended to the next floor.

Sharper's Offices

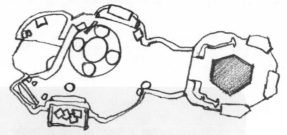

Third Journey Cloth

Third J.C. hung on office wall near elevator.

This switch opened/closed window shades.

Saw waterfall through telescope. Looked like fresh water.

The elevator brought me up to a small office above the control room. The main features of the office were a cluttered desk and a fish tank. I walked into the office and turned around to look back at the elevator, and I saw the third Journey Cloth of the Age hanging on the wall; I wasted no time in touching it.

On the wall to the left side of the desk was a lever that opened the window shutters. Opening the shutters allowed me to look through a telescope in front of one of the windows and see a waterfall in the distance.

The Desk

Sketch #1 of aquatic creature.

Sketch #2 of aquatic creature.

Sketch #3 of aquatic creature.

Sketch #4 of aquatic creature.

URU
AGES BEYOND MYST.
Prima's Official Travel Guide

I sat down at the desk and examined the papers that lay scattered across it. Most of them seemed to be sketches of some large aquatic creature, a model of which sat on the left side of the desk.

Sketch #5 of aquatic creature.

Sketch of bucket elevator.

Scribbled notes in the margins of the pages referred to the creature's surprising size. There was also a sketch of the bucket mechanism that suggested it could be turned into an elevator. All of the handwriting on the sketches was in English; this office had been used recently by a human being.

Sketch of cavern—looks important. Arabic numerals, counterclockwise from top left, are: 4, 7, 1, 5, 3, 6, 2.

Fry-Man aquarium product registration card, filled out by Douglas Sharper.

Fry-Man aquarium instructions. Hold the light button for 3 sec. to open safe, eh?

In the center of the desk was a sketch of what looked like a cavern, with the D'ni numerals 1-7 used to label seven different blocks in the cavern. I made sure to take a good photo of the sketch and translate the D'ni numerals into their Arabic equivalents; starting at the upper-left numeral and moving counterclockwise, the numbers were: 4, 7, 1, 5, 3, 6, 2.

Two pieces of paper on the desk related to the "Fry-Man" aquarium on the other side of the room. The first was the product registration card, filled out by a Douglas Sharper, who was presumably the occupant of the office. The other was a sheet of instructions describing how to open the hidden safe built into the bottom of the aquarium—simply press and hold the aquarium's light switch for at least three seconds.

Aside from the papers, the only other items on the desk were a beautiful quill pen and a helmet of unknown design. Though both seemed to be of D'ni construction, they didn't seem to serve any purpose at the present time.

Yeesha Page

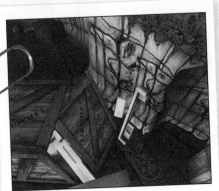

Found Yeesha Page on floor
behind crate near aquarium.

Putting page in Linking
Book added a new roof to
my Relto hut.

Having read on the aquarium instruction sheet describing a hidden safe in the base of the aquarium, I was eager to see what Douglas Sharper hid in it.

I walked over to the aquarium, but something on the floor next to the aquarium's packing crate caught my eye. It seemed to be a page from a book. I picked it up and saw that it was the same size and shape as the pages in Yeesha's Linking Book. At the top of it was a green symbol that looked like a teepee or thatched roof, and below that was the symbol I assumed was Yeesha's name in D'ni. I opened the Linking Book and placed the page inside. As I did, it seemed to meld with the spine and affix itself permanently, just after the Book's linking panel. I would realize later that this was my first "Yeesha Page," and I would see that it had made a change to Relto when I linked back there later; my hut suddenly had a new roof!

The Aquarium

Aquarium was filled with baby "Flappers."

Held light switch down for three seconds before releasing it.

Sharper hid a secret Linking Book in the aquarium safe.

Note the DRC stamp on the left page. Sharper was hoarding this one.

After collecting the Yeesha Page, I examined the aquarium, which had four of those leaping lily pad creatures that I'd seen earlier (I would read in Sharper's journal that he called them "Flappers"). The ones in the aquarium were much smaller than those outside, suggesting that they were in the early stages of their

development. It also suggested that whoever used this office had been there recently to take care of them, because the creatures were still alive and active, yet hadn't grown into adulthood yet.

As interesting as the leaping creatures were, I was more interested in seeing what Sharper had placed in the aquarium safe. As per the instructions on the desk, I pushed and held the tank's light switch for a good three seconds before releasing it.

The aquarium's base slid open to reveal a Linking Book that had a DRC stamp on the left page. I wasted no time in placing my hand on the linking panel.

Sharper's D'ni Office

My link-in point from the Linking Book in Sharper's Teledahn office.

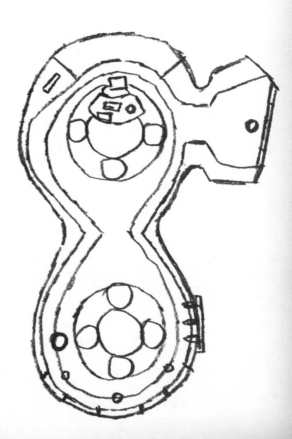

*My first glimpse of D'ni?
Taken through window in
Sharper's second office.*

*Linking Book to return to
Sharper's Teledahn office.*

I reappeared inside another office, but this one was obviously not on Teledahn.
I saw no sun at all when I looked out the window. In fact, I seemed to be in
an enormous misty underground cavern on the edge of a vast city that had been
built around a huge underground lake. Could this be D'ni?

I couldn't see much from the two windows in the office, and the telescope
in front of one didn't have much range of motion at all. But from my limited
field of vision, everything seemed to match the descriptions of D'ni that I'd
read. This meant that I was on Earth, albeit deep underground. It was a
comforting thought, even though there seemed to be no way to leave the office
except through a Linking Book on a pedestal that showed an image of the
Teledahn office in its linking panel. Three paintings of Teledahn landscapes
hung on the rounded wall.

The Desk

Another desk, littered with papers. Found some interesting stuff here.

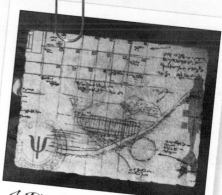

A D'ni language sketch, found on desk. An identical one hung on the wall.

Sketches of gears and wheels. Sharper's design ideas? Or older?

Doodles on this notepad looked like ideas for Teledahn basket elevator.

I sat down at the office desk to look at the papers and journals covering its smooth stone surface. There were three sketches, one of which was a reproduction of a D'ni-language sketch that hung on the wall. The other two looked like sketches of machines; one may have been a sheet of ideas for the proposed basket elevator in Teledahn.

The remaining sheet of paper was a short note addressed to Dr. Watson from someone named "Marie."

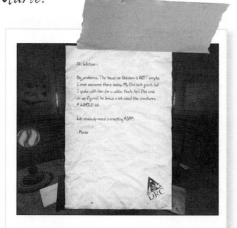

This letter from Marie to Dr. Watson mentioned "creatures" and a D'ni survivor.

Dr. Watson—

Big problems. The house of Noloben is _not_ empty. I met someone there today. My D'ni isn't great, but I spoke with him for a while. Yeah, he's D'ni and, as we figured, he knows a lot about the creatures. _A whole lot._

We obviously need a meeting AS AP.

—Marie

Sharper's journal was filled with all sorts of useful information. Must copy it.

So there was at least one D'ni survivor, and the DRC had made contact with him! But what were these "creatures" that Marie wrote about? Obviously, she and Dr. Watson were familiar with them, and for the first time since I saw the image of Yeesha, I felt as if perhaps waiting for Dr. Watson and visiting D'ni with the DRC might not have been such a bad idea. But, because I had no way to

return to the Cleft, there was no point in thinking about that now.

The remaining item of note on the desk was perhaps the most important: Douglas Sharper's personal journal.

EDITOR'S NOTE:
The entire contents of Douglas Sharper's journal are reprinted in "Appendix B: DRC Research" at the end of this book.

Linking Stone

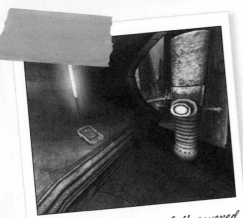

Found a mysterious cloth-covered stone next to the telescope.

Stone looked like a cross between a Journey Page and a linking Page.

After reading Sharper's journal, I examined the only other item of interest in the office: a cloth-covered stone hanging on the wall near the telescope. I'd never seen or read about anything like it. The cloth resembled the same burlap material that the Journey Cloths were made of, right down to the frayed red border. Was this another of Yeesha's unconventional creations?

The Yeesha connection was made more obvious when I looked at the small symbol etched into the lower-right corner of the stone. It showed a humanoid figure receiving a Linking Book from an outstretched hand, which resembled the hand rune on the Journey Cloths and Relto pedestals . . . or perhaps the hand was receiving the Linking Book from the humanoid figure? What was that hand symbol meant to represent? I'd seen it on several items on Yeesha's quest, but it didn't seem to represent Yeesha herself, since she had her own rune.

The shape of a page had been sculpted into the center of the stone in precise lines that contrasted with the rough-hewn look of the rest of the object. In the center of the page was what looked like a linking panel. I decided to place my hand on it and see what happened.

Back to Teledahn

Touched the stone's linking panel and wound up on a mushroom stump in Teledahn.

Had to link back to Relto to leave the stump.

Sure enough, the stone functioned exactly like a linking Page, and I reappeared on Teledahn atop the stump of a giant mushroom that had been cut down. The stump overlooked the part of Teledahn that I'd traveled through before.

I quickly realized that there was no way to leave the stump. Even with a running jump, I couldn't clear the wall around it (and even if I had been able to, I would've wound up in the swamp).

Used Teledahn Linking Book's Journey Cloth bookmark to return to Sharper's Teledahn office.

Fortunately, I still had Yeesha's Linking Book, so I linked back to Relto and pulled out the Teledahn Linking Book from my Library. By placing my hand on the Journey Cloth bookmark, I linked directly into the Teledahn office, the location of the last Journey Cloth I'd touched in Teledahn.

Pressed elevator's brown button to go back down to cabin.

Return to the Cabin

I'd seen everything there was to see in the Teledahn office and in Sharper's secret D'ni office, so I got back in the elevator and pressed the left brown button to return to the control room. Pressing the brown button again brought me back down to the cabin, where I'd begun my Teledahn exploration.

That lever on the control panel <u>did</u> drain the water around here.

The control panel switch unlocked the cabin floor grate.

I saw that the water that had previously surrounded the cabin had indeed drained when I pulled the lever in the center of the control panel upstairs. I remembered that I'd also flipped a switch that seemed to be the unlocking mechanism for the grated hatch in the floor of the cabin.

A red light glowed underneath the handle of the hatch, a promising sign. I pulled on it and found that I had indeed unlocked the hatch, and it opened to reveal a ladder leading down to a lower floor.

The Storm Drain

Prima's Official Trav...

Climbed down two long ladders beneath the cabin's hatch.

The first of three pictograms in storm drain—slaves?

Saw this one a little farther up. No idea what it means.

Third pictogram at end of drain. Didn't understand this one either.

I climbed down the ladder, which must have been at least 30 feet long, until I reached the bottom of what had been the water reservoir. Another ladder led down farther below the reservoir floor; I stepped onto this and began my descent.

The second ladder was at least as long as the first, and it ended in a huge storm drain. I ran through the ankle-deep water until I reached a gap in the right side of the drain. Next to the gap was a crude pictogram of three figures, two of which seemed to be chained together at the feet. Could this be a reference to the slave caverns I'd read about in Sharper's journal?

I saw two other pictograms along the walls of the drain, but I couldn't make any sense of them (though I did make sure to photograph them). The end of the drain curved upward too steeply for me to climb out of it, so I returned to the gap in the pipe, went through it, and up the stairs beyond it.

Slave Cavern

Fourth Journey Cloth

Slave cavern. Don't even want to think about what happened here.

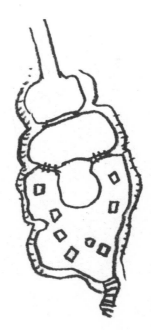

Prima's Official Travel Guide

A long cavern stretched out from the top of the stairs. Bones, rocks, and other debris lay scattered along the floor of it. Seven metal plates had been fitted into the floor. Each plate depressed when I stepped on it, then raised again after I removed my weight. I had the sickening feeling that this is what Sharper was talking about in his journal

Fourth journey cloth hung on wall near entrance.

when he referred to the slaves that Manesmo was supposed to have kept.

The fourth Journey Cloth hung on the wall of the cavern. I touched it and reflected on the significance of the Journey Cloths; if Yeesha meant them to represent stages of a journey, does this mean that I was following in the footsteps of someone who had been enslaved by the D'ni?

Pressure Plates

Seven switches in the cavern beyond—some kind of combination? #'s 2, 4, 6, and 7 are up (active?).

Seven pressure plates in the floor. Rocks could keep them pressed down. . . .

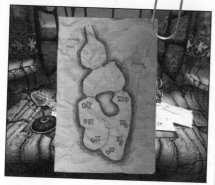

Cavern sketch from Sharper's desk. Counterclockwise from upper left, plates are numbered: 4, 7, 1, 5, 3, 6, 2.

Two locked gates at the far end of the cavern prevented me from going any farther. Looking through the gates, I saw another gate—this one open—in the cavern beyond. Next to that open gate were what looked like seven switches, each of which had a raised yellow or lowered gray panel above it. Switches 2, 4, 6, and 7 were yellow and raised; switches 1, 3, and 5 were gray and lowered.

Seven switches, seven pressure plates—they were obviously related somehow. It was then that I remembered the cavern sketch on Sharper's Teledahn office desk. I took a look at it and saw that it described the cavern perfectly. It also conveniently numbered the pressure plates for me. I deduced that the switches in the far cavern corresponded to the pressure plates in the cavern I was in, like some sort of combination lock, perhaps.

Used Sharper's sketch to number plates and weigh them down. This was #2

After a bit of trial and error, I figured out that the secret to the pressure plates was to weigh down the correct plates as indicated by the raised yellow switches in the cavern beyond. Plates 2, 4, 6, 7 had to be triggered, and all four plates had to be weighted down to operate the mechanism.

Plate #6

Plate #7

Plate #4

So, as I stood in the entrance to the cavern and faced the locked gates, I realized that I had to depress the four pressure plates farthest from me, two at the far right end of the cavern and two at the far left end. The rocks and larger bones scattered throughout the cavern were heavy enough to do the trick, so I kicked them onto the plates in the proper order.

As I went about my task, I noticed etched into the floor between pressure plates 6 and 7 the symbol I'd come to associate with Yeesha, but I didn't have any idea how this was significant. Was it a clue from Yeesha, or did the symbol represent something else altogether?

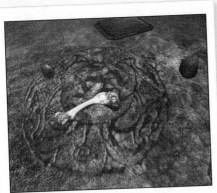

Another occurrence of the "Yeesha symbol" ?

1st chamber's gates opened (and stayed open) once all four plates were weighted down . . .

. . . but 2nd chamber's gate closed when 1st chamber's opened.

Switches seemed to determine pressure plate combination. What if I change the combo?

As I pushed the last rock onto pressure plate 7, the gates slid open, and I ran through them, fearing that they might shut behind me. Fortunately, they didn't.

Changing switch combo closed 1st chamber's gates (because pressure plates were no longer right) and opened 2nd chamber's.

However, as soon as the gates opened in the first chamber of the cavern, the open gate in the second chamber closed. I realized that this must have been a safety feature for the slavers—even if the slaves in the first chamber could figure out the pressure plate combination, they wouldn't make it past the second chamber before guards could be called.

I looked at the array of seven switches in the second chamber. As an experiment, I touched one below a raised yellow panel, flipping the panel over to its gray side. The first chamber's gates slammed shut, and the second chamber's gate opened. After doing it, I realized that the switches did in fact determine the pressure plate combination, and changing the switches changed the combination, which returned the gates to their original positions.

Beyond the Slave Caverns

Ah, fresh air again! That's the waterfall I saw from Sharper's Teledahn office.

A whole bunch of Flappers around here. Sharper mentioned in his journal that they were Shroomie's favorite snacks.

Stupid raised platform! Take that!

Wow, my jump-kick worked! Pulling lever lowered it the rest of the way.

I was pretty pleased with myself for figuring out the solution to the puzzle, but I was even more pleased that I could now go through the second chamber's gate and into the cavern beyond it.

The cavern ended in an outdoor walkway that ran along the outer wall of the slave cavern. Flappers leapt up and down on the surface of the swamp, and in the distance, I saw the waterfall that I'd seen through the telescope in Sharper's Teledahn office.

I headed down the walkway past more Flappers until I came to a raised section of the walkway that kept me from going any farther. Pulling the lever in front of it didn't seem to do anything.

Spore dispenser?
Shroomie feeder?

I had just about run out of clever ideas, so I ran toward the raised walkway and jumped into it. To my surprise, my frustration actually paid off, and I managed to knock the walkway down to a 45-degree angle. I pulled the lever again, and this time, the walkway lowered into position.

Just beyond the walkway, another lever activated a mechanism that sprinkled spores over the top of the water. I wondered if this was something that Sharper had built to attract the Flappers in order to lure his beloved Shroomie. It didn't seem to do its job, if that was the point of it. Then again, the water was so stagnant that I would have been surprised if anything besides those weird Flappers was able to survive in it.

Fifth Journey Cloth

Stairs at end of walkway led up to plateau.

Used crates to get up to rock ledge with fifth Journey Cloth on it.

I walked to the end of the pathway and climbed up a set of stone stairs at the end of it. Looking back, I saw that I was now behind the power tower, in a part of Teledahn that I hadn't seen yet.

The stairs led to an open plateau, with stacked crates and a door to the right. As I approached the door, something on the stone ledge above it caught my eye—another Journey Cloth! I jumped up onto the crates to the right of the door to reach the ledge, and then I jumped across the gap in the ledge above the door to reach the Journey Cloth.

Ladder near J.C. was too high to reach. Come back after I figure out how to lower it. (This shot took forever to set up!)

I touched the Journey Cloth and breathed a sigh of relief; now if I had to link away from Teledahn, I could link directly back to this spot via the Journey Cloth bookmark and not have to deal with the pressure plates in the slave cavern. Actually, to be quite honest, the pressure plates weren't the worst part of that cavern; the knowledge of what must have happened there before the fall of D'ni was far, far worse.

I walked along the rest of the narrow ledge, but there was nowhere else to go. I did, however, see a retracted ladder overhead and several boulders hanging from ropes. Even after several minutes of examination, I couldn't figure out how to get up to the ladder without breaking my neck, so I walked back to the door below the ledge and went through it.

Second Linking Stone

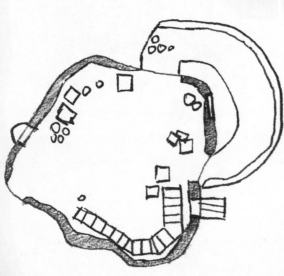

Door was unlocked. Decided to make myself at home.

Another copy of that chart.
What did it mean?

Found another Linking Stone
behind some crates. Should
have waited to use it until
after Gahreesen.

The room on the other side of the door had
stacked crates along the floor, two sketches
hanging on the wall, and a metal pathway
that reached up to another door. I recognized
both sketches from Sharper's D'ni office.
One seemed to show several views of the
Shroomie creature, and the other might have
been some sort of calendar or chart, but I
couldn't figure it out.

Door at top of metal walkway
was also unlocked. Went through
it to continue exploration.

    While poking around the crates, I
found another one of those Linking
Stones, similar to the one I found in Sharper's D'ni office.
Although I did use it to link when I first found it, I realized later that my
experiences on the other end of that link were actually a part of my Gahreesen
Age exploration, so I decided against describing those events in this chapter.

EDITOR'S NOTE:
For more information on this Linking Stone, see the "Gahreesen Prisons" chapter of this guide.)

Hand-Print Door and Sixth Journey Cloth

Another "hand-print" door—probably won't open 'til I find all seven Journey Cloths.

Journey Cloth #6 was right across from the door.

Cavern beyond J.C. #6 looked promising. Decided to investigate.

Continuing my exploration of Teledahn, I passed through the door at the end of the metal walkway and entered a large cave lit by a pulsing amber light at its center.

The first object of interest I saw here was a door to my right, which had the palm symbol in the center of it.

Remembering the door in the base of the tree in the Cleft, I realized that I would have to find all seven Journey Cloths before I could open it, and I still had two to go.

Just beyond that door, on the left side of the cave, was the sixth Journey Cloth. If I could just find one more, I could enter that door, which I assumed would be the end of my Teledahn Journey, just as the similar door in the Cleft ended my Cleft Journey. I activated the Journey Cloth and headed down the tunnel to the right of the cloth.

Mining Gun

Looked like the power tower's periscope was actually a mining gun.

Powerful enough to put a hole in that big hunk of metal.

The tunnel ended in another metal walkway overlooking the freshwater area of Teledahn. Halfway down the walkway was a periscope that resembled the one on the power tower.

I looked through it and saw that it had the same directional control buttons as the power tower periscope, but with two additional controls: a sliding knob in the lower-right corner that controlled the lens' zoom, and a flashing blue button that fired some sort of projectile into the center of the

viewfinder (I accidentally put a few holes into the side of a hulking piece of machinery before I figured that out—then I put a few more in it!). This must have been the mining gun that Sharper referred to in his journal.

I used the mining gun to get a better view of my surroundings, including the area where I found the fifth Journey Cloth. I could also see that the ladder near the Journey Cloth that I'd been unable to reach was suspended from ropes just like the hanging boulders that surrounded it. Could this be some sort of counterweight system?

Smashing counterweight boulder dropped hanging ladder near J.C. #5.

Shattered hanging boulders near Journey Cloth #5 and had fun doing it.

Another Shroomie feeder. Still no Shroomie.

Because I had access to the mining gun (and because I was kind of enjoying my target practice), I decided to see if I could hit the hanging boulders. It turned out that I could! With each successful shot, the boulders flew apart.

After shattering one of them, the hanging ladder dropped to the ledge where I'd found the fifth Journey Cloth. So it <u>was</u> a counterweight system after all! I made a mental note to return later and investigate.

I walked down to the end of the metal pathway, where I found another spore-dispensing device that I thought may have been used to lure Shroomie. Seeing it in proximity to the mining gun made me understand something I'd read in Sharper's journal—he didn't just study the Shroomies; he hunted them as well. I pulled the handle, but nothing happened. Had Sharper hunted them to extinction?

Shroomie Gate

Backtracked into cave and took a left to reach "Shroomie Gate" lever.

Pulling lever opened gate between industrial and freshwater areas of Teledahn.

Jumped on end of walkway to lower it to mushroom. Created path directly to power tower.

I returned to the cavern with the sixth Journey Cloth and turned left at the end of the small tunnel I'd just come through. This brought me to yet another metal walkway.

Directly in front of me was a lever, and just past that was an enormous metal gate that divided the industrialized part of Teledahn from the placid freshwater part of the Age. It didn't take a rocket scientist to figure out that pulling the lever would open the gate, and that's exactly what I did.

The walkway extended to the right and would have run straight up to the power tower, but it had somehow been damaged, possibly by a falling mushroom. The other end rested on top of a mushroom cap, but the section I was on was too high for me to safely cross onto the mushroom below it. A reckless idea came into my head, and I jumped up and landed on the walkway with all of my weight. The walkway creaked under me and lowered just enough so that I could run onto the mushroom, giving me a handy shortcut to the power tower.

Seventh Journey Cloth

Backtracked to rock ledge with
Journey Cloth #5 on it to reach
ladder I lowered. (Another
tricky photo to set up!)

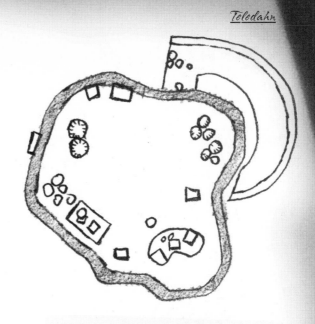

Climbed ladder to reach office
with 7th Journey Cloth in it.

Stairs led down to hidden door
in room below. Nice
backtracking shortcut.

I backtracked through the cave with the sixth Journey Cloth, through the round
room with the metal walkway, and out to the plateau where I'd found the fifth
Journey Cloth. I hopped up on the crates to the right of the door and climbed up
onto the ledge, just as I'd done when I got the fifth Journey Cloth.

I was now able to climb up the formerly out-of-reach ladder because I had shattered its counterweight boulder with the mining gun. At the top of the ladder was a round office of sorts, with some scattered furnishings and the final Journey Cloth.

After touching the Journey Cloth, I walked through an open doorway and down a set of stairs. I ran my hand along it until I found a hidden catch that dropped it to the floor, revealing a secret door into the room below—the round room with the metal walkway.

Bahro Cave Door

From this room, I returned to the door with the hand print on it. Before I touched the door, I touched the nearby Journey Cloth again. Even though I had touched the Cloth earlier, I wanted to make sure that I could link directly back to this cavern from the Teledahn Linking Book in Relto if anything went wrong.

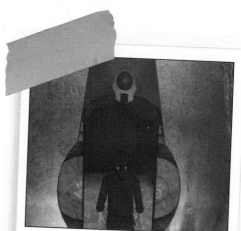

After getting all seven Journey Cloths, the hand-print (Bahro Cave) door opened.

With that done, I approached the door and touched it. Just as the door in the Cleft had opened after I found all seven Journey Cloths, so did this one. I stepped into the blackest cave I'd ever seen and continued fumbling forward until I felt the curious sensation of linking transport me to another place.

Bahro Cave

Yeesha's Voice

I reappeared on a rock shelf in a cavern dimly lit by the blue light of overhead censers. In front of me was something that looked like a totem pole and pulsed with the same blue light as the runes in the Cleft cavern. A D'ni symbol, similar to those on the Cleft Imager, was etched into the ground. Three more pillars sat on three more rock ledges, none of which I could reach.

Walking through hand-print door linked me to this weird blue cave.

As soon as I arrived, I heard Yeesha's voice echoing in the chamber:

"Your journey has begun. You can't imagine how these small things affect the future, but someday you will. You will return.

"Many paths have brought me to this place: The path of my great-grandmother, bringer of destruction. The path of my grandfather, the rebuilder of pride. The path of my mother, writer of dreams. And of my father—my dear father—the caretaker of burdens.

"And I knew that at the end of such great paths must lay a great purpose. I returned to the Cleft to find it.

"The Cleft, the fissure in the desert, the wound in the Earth, the path to things beneath the surface—it was there I sought to find my purpose. It was from there I came to know the dead underground city of D'ni.

"These D'ni people, who are now gone, came thousands of years ago to the shelter of the cavern to return to leastness. They found solace in their smallness in the dark, and so did I.

"But light is powerful in the darkness.

"Did you see the hidden caves and the cages? It is where the proud would keep the Least. The Least were only animals after all—animals that could link. They could be put to work or play, they could ease the burden of the proud, and fill their free time with entertainment. Quietly as D'ni slept, their lives were taken, because the proud make the rules.

"This wasn't the first time such a blasphemy was part of D'ni. The D'ni histories whisper of it. Like Va'tuhg the Ager, or King Asemlef. And even in this Age, it may not be the last.

"And now to these Pillars. These four Pillars around you are the very being of the Bahro. You must take them. They will bring a great treasure to Relto, your Age, the island in the clouds. Relto will be their keeper for only a brief time."

Touching this symbol played Yeesha's speech again.

Yeesha's voice faded, as did the glow from a symbol on the wall. Examining the symbol, I saw that it resembled one from the Cleft cavern: a humanoid figure holding a staff or pole. Above the figure was the rune I guessed was Yeesha's name. I touched the symbol, and Yeesha's voice repeated the speech I had just heard.

Answers and Questions

As I listened to her speech a second time, recording it for transcription later, I found that some of my questions were answered, but I was left with many more.

I found it strange that Yeesha referred to her great-grandmother, Anna, as the "bringer of destruction," because it was a commonly accepted historical fact that two D'ni, Veovis and A'Geris, were the ones who unleashed the plague that destroyed D'ni. True, both The Book of Atrus and The Book of Ti'ana described how Anna pleaded before the D'ni council to commute a death sentence for Veovis to one of life imprisonment, allowing him to return and carry out his genocidal plans. But those D'ni survivors who blamed Anna for the destruction of D'ni tended to be less-than-savory characters, such as her son, Gehn.

And while I was a bit disturbed by Yeesha's opinion of her great-grandmother, I was reassured by the fact that she referred to Gehn, her grandfather, as "the rebuilder of pride." In the two speeches I'd heard from her, Yeesha did not seem to view pride as a positive virtue.

In fact, I was now reasonably certain that she viewed most or all D'ni as overly prideful and deserving of their fate. That "blame the victim" mentality made me feel more than a bit uneasy, but after hearing what Yeesha had to say about the slave pens—not to mention my own observation of them—I found it hard to find her opinion of D'ni wholly without merit.

I also thought that I was starting to understand her story and my journey a bit more. She referred to the slaves in Teledahn as "the Least," viewed by the D'ni as "animals that could link." Was Yeesha's association with these "Least" the source of her unconventional writing ability that allowed her to violate the D'ni linking laws? Did they have something to do with the Linking Stones that I had seen in Teledahn?

And who were these people, exactly? Yeesha used a word I didn't recognize when she was describing the glowing Pillars; she said that the Pillars were "the very being of the Bahro." What exactly did that mean? I'd read the word "bahro" in one of the Myst novels, but I couldn't recall its meaning at the moment. Were these "Bahro" the slaves that were treated like animals by the D'ni?

The Bahro Pillar

Yeesha referred to this pillar as "the very being of the Bahro," whoever it/they are.

Touching hand symbol caused Bahro Pillar to vanish (to Relto?).

Uh-oh. Linking Book's on the fritz.

Despite the fact that I still wasn't sure exactly what was going on, I continued to muddle through until things started making sense. On the wall of the cavern, next to the Yeesha symbol, was the hand symbol. Every time I'd seen one of these, I'd touched it and made something happen, so I figured there wasn't any reason to break with tradition.

I placed my hand on the symbol, and the Bahro Pillar disappeared. Yeesha said something about bringing the Pillars to Relto—was that what just happened? There was only one way to find out. I opened the Linking Book on my hip and laid my hand on the linking panel.

Nothing happened. I tried linking again but to no avail. The linking panel showed only a dark, swirling cloud. How was I going to get out of here? Touching the hand icon again only returned the Bahro Pillar to its original position, and I was pretty sure that wasn't going to help. I removed the Pillar again and tried not to panic.

Leaving the Cave

My God. It's full of stars.

Took this one with my eyes shut tight.

I looked down over the edge of the rock shelf I was on to see a vast starry expanse below me that took my breath away. These starry fissures were a recurring theme

in the <u>Myst</u> stories, especially the one in Riven, into which Atrus threw his Myst Linking Book to keep it out of Gehn's hands. Was I supposed to . . . jump into this one?

I spent what seemed like an hour trying to find any other way to get out of this cavern, but there was simply nothing else to do. I decided that I would try to leap to one of the other stone ledges. They were obviously out of my range, but I couldn't convince myself to just leap blindly into the starry void below.

Taking a deep breath, I steeled my nerves and ran directly toward the nearest ledge. I leapt into the air, and for a second I thought I might make the jump. As I began the declining arc of my leap, however, it became obvious that I was going to be at least a couple of feet short.

I watched the ledge sail by overhead as I plunged into the void. I didn't even have time to scream before I felt my body disappear into nothingness.

Return to Relto

Whew! Safe and sound in Relto. Bahro Pillar appeared on top of the pillar that held Teledahn Linking Book.

To my great relief, I reappeared on Relto along with the Bahro Pillar, which was inserted into the pedestal that housed the Teledahn Linking Book. The pedestal sunk into the ground, continuing to emit its pulsing blue glow.

Exhausted, I dropped to the ground as well, my heart still racing, my entire body shaking. Would it have killed Yeesha to tell me how to get out of that damn cave?

Gahreesen
Linking to Gahreesen

Gahreesen pedestal—far left pedestal from the hut entrance.

Touched hand print to reveal Linking Book.

After completing my journey through Teledahn, I took what I considered to be a well-deserved rest. Upon awakening, I picked out a fresh change of clothes from the Relto hut's closet and prepared to link to the next Age on my itinerary: Gahreesen.

As I stood in the doorway and consulted my notes, I saw that the Gahreesen Linking Book was stored in the far-left pedestal. I approached the pedestal and touched the hand-print icon to open the pedestal and take the Linking Book.

Opening the Linking Book, I took a deep breath and placed my hand on the Linking Panel. Once again, I felt myself falling into the ever-expanding page as Relto dissolved around me.

URU
AGES BEYOND MYST.
Prima's Official Travel Guide

NOTE

Before I begin to describe Gahreesen, I want to mention that many of the ideas and observations expressed in the following pages come from the journal of a DRC member named Simpson, who spent seven months exploring Gahreesen in 2001 and 2002. I found the journal near the end of my exploration of Gahreesen, but for clarity's sake, I've incorporated many of its more salient points into my initial observations of the Age. All of the names of the various areas of Gahreesen come from Simpson's journal.

Entrance

Entrance room; link-in point of Gahreesen.

Maintainer symbol: an open eye over an open book.

According to Simpson's journal, Gahreesen was designed for security and was used primarily by a "special forces" branch of the D'ni Guild of Maintainers. Maintainers were the closest thing that the D'ni had to a traditional law-enforcement organization. From what I had read of them previously, the Maintainers primarily concerned

themselves with the stability and safety of Ages and ensured that the laws governing the interaction of the D'ni with non-D'ni were followed. There weren't many mentions of the Maintainers having to deal with internal D'ni conflicts.

The Maintainers' symbol was an unblinking eye suspended over an open book, representing their eternal vigilance over the Ages. The symbol appeared everywhere in Gahreesen (Simpson noted sarcastically that this might have been so that you didn't forget where you were).

The entrance was designed for maximum security: thick stone walls, one door, and an observation window high overhead (which Simpson implied might have actually been a sniper post). Even if anyone managed to reach the book and link in, they wouldn't have been able to cause much damage to this room.

As soon as I linked into the Age, I heard the low rumble of heavy machinery. A pattern of sunlight, filtered through the open roof of the room, drifted in a slow circle around the walls. I figured that Gahreesen, like Teledahn, must have had a fast-moving sun, but I wouldn't realize until later that I was in error.

Because there was only one way to go, I headed through the open doorway into the Waiting Room.

"Please retrieve your KI."

Waiting Room

The small Waiting Room had two thick stone doors and two grated windows. As I walked through the door from the entrance, I saw a sign next to the door directly in

Window to Locker Room.

Window to Beetle Cages.

front of me. At the top of the sign was the DRC stamp, and it requested the reader to "Please retrieve your KI." A drawing of an object that looked like a stopwatch appeared at the bottom of the sign, with an arrow pointing to the right, down the hallway beyond the door. (Simpson noted in his journal that the two doors of the Waiting Room were designed so that they could never be open simultaneously, but it seemed as if the DRC had found a way to circumvent that, because both were open.)

Though I couldn't fathom the purpose of the two windows in the Waiting Room when I first visited it, Simpson's journal clarified their purposes. The window to the right was designed so that any restricted material (such as Linking Books) could be held securely while its owner visited Gahreesen.

The other window, which was formed in the stylized symbol of a beetle, was another security device. Simpson's journal noted that the room beyond the window was filled with cages that once held a special kind of beetle that sniffed out Linking Book ink like a bloodhound. If anyone tried to sneak in with a Linking Book, the beetles would swarm through this window, alerting the guards. Fortunately for me, the beetles were long gone, probably sometime shortly after the fall of D'ni more than 200 years ago.

Hall

Hall ran around the entire circumference of the building.

DRC safety cones blocked locked door at end of hall; went through open door near cones.

It seemed as if thick stone halls ran around the entire circumference of the building. The DRC had placed road cones and a sawhorse to the left of the exit from the Waiting Room. I could easily move past them, but because the stone door beyond them was locked, I didn't see much point in doing so.

Instead, I turned right (in the direction that the DRC sign's arrow pointed) and followed the hall through another open door. I noted that the walls of the hall were just as solid as the walls of the entrance, and they were so narrow that it

would be hard to fight your way through them. To top it all off, there were huge stone doors every 30 feet or so, which would have allowed the Maintainers to easily trap anyone who decided to misbehave in them.

The hallway extended beyond the open doorway, at the end of which were more road cones and another sawhorse in front of a sealed stone door. Fortunately, an open door was directly in front of the cones. This led to the Locker Room.

Locker Room

Locker Room window into Waiting Room.

Locker Room, where restricted items were stored.

The Locker Room was so named because it was where the Maintainers stored any restricted items carried by visitors into the Waiting Room.

Diamond-shaped lockers lined the walls of the room, and an open door admitted entry to the room to the left.

By turning right after entering the Locker Room, I saw the Waiting Room window and the DRC sign beyond it.

Linking Stone

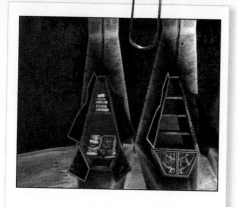

Found Linking Stone in locker near Waiting Room window.

Looked like a cross between a Linking Page and a Journey Cloth.

As I turned away from the Waiting Room window, something in the locker to my right caught my eye. I took a closer look and found another one of those cloth-covered Linking Stones that I'd seen in Teledahn. Because I hadn't explored much of Gahreesen yet, and since it would take all of about two minutes to retrace my progress from Relto, I placed my hand on the Linking Stone and felt myself disappear from Gahreesen.

I reappeared on a balcony in another Age, which I was absolutely convinced was the great city, D'ni. The balcony overlooked one of the ancient neighborhoods, dimly lit by a pale yellow light. In the distance was the cavern's underground lake, which glowed a faint orange from the phosphorescent algae that lived in it.

For a moment, I regretted skipping out on my meeting with Dr. Watson. The DRC explored D'ni freely, having had access to the city's wonders and secrets for several years now. Were I affiliated with them, I would be walking those streets now, not just looking at them from above.

Stone slab blocked balcony door.
What did the etchings mean?

Linking Stone brought me to a
D'ni city balcony.

It didn't take me long to realize that there
was no way to leave the balcony without
linking away from it. It was too far to drop from,
and a giant stone slab blocked the door that led onto it.

The slab had a series of engravings on it, and it was trying to tell a story. If
Yeesha intended me to find that Linking Stone in Gahreesen (and I believed that
she did), then there was definitely a reason for me to see this slab. Without much
formal training in archaeological study, however, I'm afraid that much of its
meaning was lost on me.

The lower-left corner of the slab seemed to describe the Bahro Cave that I'd
visited at the end of the Teledahn journey. It had what looked like four Bahro
Pillars in it and a field of stars underneath it.

The image at the top of the slab showed a rocky island jutting up from the
clouds. Perched atop the island was a hut. It was supposed to be Relto; I was
almost sure of that. Lines drawn from a Bahro Pillar above the Bahro Cave
implied the transfer of the Pillar from the Cave to Relto, as I had done at the end
of the Teledahn journey. That much was clear after a few minutes of study.

The etchings on the right side of the slab confused me, however. They seemed to indicate another cave with four more Pillars and clouds rather than a starry field beneath it. Four figures stood underneath the second cave's Pillars—were these meant to be the Bahro? If so, what did it all mean?

I felt as if I'd deciphered as much of the slab as I was capable of doing at the moment. I studied it until I'd memorized its every detail, and then I took a couple of photos of it for further study before linking back to Relto.

Had to link back to Relto to leave balcony.

KI Dispenser

Gahreesen Linking Book appeared in my Library; book farthest to the left.

Returned to Locker Room and went through open door into next room.

After linking back to Relto, I entered the hut and picked up the leftmost Linking Book in my Library, which had the Maintainers' seal on the spine. Placing my hand on the Linking Panel, I transported back to Gahreesen and returned to the Locker Room.

The open door to the left of the Locker Room entrance brought me to a room with more traffic cones and a machine with a blue light in the center of it. I approached the device and saw that it was engraved with the same symbol that I'd seen on the DRC sign in the Waiting Room. This was apparently where I would get my "KI," whatever that was.

The KI Dispenser. Placing my hand under it gave me a KI.

I placed my hand under the glowing blue circle in the center of the machine, and a small device about the size and shape of a wristwatch fell into my hand. I slipped it around my hand and took a look at it. It was definitely of D'ni construction, but the DRC was encouraging its explorers to pick them up. For the second time today, I felt as if I might have been missing something by not joining up with the DRC.

Next to the KI Dispenser were more traffic cones, with an open door beyond them. I realized that there was one big advantage to not being a member of the DRC: you didn't have to pay any attention to their stupid traffic cones. I walked right past them to the door beyond.

Ignored safety cones and walked past them through open door beyond.

Warehouse

Simpson described a "Warehouse" room in his journal, and this room fit his description the best. It looked as if the DRC had removed most of the items in it for further study.

It also turned out that the DRC had a good reason for putting up the safety barrier in front of the entrance to this room; a huge crack ran along the middle of the floor, revealing a gap about 15 feet deep. I was honestly quite surprised to see such a thing. From what I knew

Was this Simpson's "Warehouse" room? It had seen better days.

of the D'ni, they were skilled craftsmen who built their structures to last hundreds, if not thousands, of years. I would have thought that this structure, which was designed to be so impenetrable, would have been even sturdier than most. Was this devastation caused by a natural disaster, or was it something else?

YEESHA PAGE

I saw an open door on the other side of the crack, and I decided to try leaping to the room's other side. It wasn't too far to jump, but I mistimed my first attempt and fell right into the gap in the floor.

Tried to leap gap but slipped and fell into it.

Had to link back to Relto to leave gap and then link back to Gahreesen.

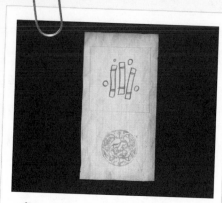

Found Yeesha Page in gap, so it wasn't a total washout.

After taking a moment to make sure that I hadn't injured myself, I saw something lying on the ground—another Yeesha Page! I picked it up and added it to my Linking Book, where it fused with the other pages as if it had always been a part of it.

I examined every nook and cranny of the gap and tried to find a way out of it, but to no avail. With a sigh, I opened my Linking Book and linked back to Relto. This was getting to be a habit, and I hoped it wouldn't happen too many more times.

Successfully leaped gap on second attempt. Nice rubble on other side.

Leapt over rubble at far end of room and found Journey Cloth.

After reappearing on Relto, I took a moment to check out the logs and rocks that the Yeesha Page had added to the ground in front of my hut, and then I linked back to Gahreesen and retraced my steps to the room with the giant gap in the floor.

This time, I got a running start and leaped over the gap successfully. Before going through the open door on the other side, I climbed over the rubble at the end of the room and was rewarded with the first Journey Cloth of the Gahreesen Age.

Beetle Cages

After getting the first Journey Cloth, I hopped back over the rubble and exited the Warehouse room through the open door, returning to the hall that ran around the perimeter of the building.

Open door from Warehouse led back into hall.

Crack in wall led into
Beetle Cages.

These bugs were either huge, or
there were a lot of them. Yuck.

I continued through an open door into another part of the hallway but was dismayed to see that the door at the end was sealed.

Fortunately, the cave-in had breached the hall's inner wall and provided an opening into the Beetle Cages. (Simpson noted in his journal that if it wasn't for the cave-in, no one would be able to access the Beetle Cages without a Linking Book, because there were no other entrances to the room. However, it seemed as if you could reach it from the room where I found the first Journey Cloth, but maybe I'm wrong about that.)

To the left of the room's entrance was the window to the Waiting Room. To the right was more rubble from the cave-in. Cages lined the walls of the room. The beetles that once inhabited them were either extremely large, or the Maintainers kept a lot of them, judging from the size and number of cages.

I hate bugs.

SECOND JOURNEY CLOTH

Between the stacks of cages were rusted rows of metal bars that could be climbed like ladders. I climbed the ladder across from the entrance to the room to reach the shelf above the cages, and I found the second Journey Cloth of the Age hanging on the wall up there.

Climbed bars between Beetle Cages to reach top of them.

Journey Cloth hung over Beetle Cages opposite entrance.

A way up to the second floor?

From my vantage point atop the cages, I saw that if I climbed the ladder on the other side of the room, I could reach a plank that extended to an upstairs room through a giant hole in the wall.

Climbed onto other set of Beetle Cages. Plank looked sturdy enough to step on.

Had to leap up ruined section of wall to reach ledge w/safety cones on it.

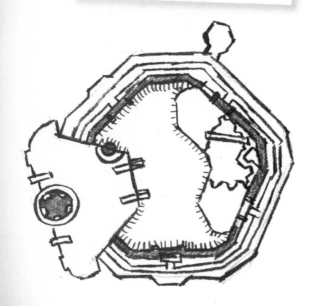

Moved very, very carefully across plank to reach 2nd floor ledge.

Reaching the second floor of the building was more than a bit of a chore. I climbed up the other set of Beetle Cages and walked along the tops of them until I reached the plank that led up to the ruins of the wall.

From there, I had to jump up the remains of the wall to reach a ledge with two orange road cones on it. Apparently the DRC considered this place dangerous. Imagine that.

Another board stretched across a gap in the second floor. A pair of road cones stood sentry at either end of the board. Below I could see the room where I found the first Journey Cloth. Moving very carefully, I stepped onto the board, accidentally kicking one of the road cones down into the room below me. The dull thump of its impact on the floor below did nothing to steady my nerves.

I crossed the board, slowly and carefully. I figured that I could probably fall off of it without being hurt too badly, but I didn't even want to chance it. Fortunately, I made it to the other side without incident.

I looked out the window on the other side of the board and realized that I was standing in the observation room (or, if Simpson was correct, the sniper post) that overlooked the entrance to Gahreesen.

Rotating Wall

Crack in hallway wall revealed rotating wall, which had a gap in it.

Pressed up against rotating wall and ran into gap when it came around.

A gap in the wall opposite the observation window led into the second-floor hallway, which was almost identical to the first-floor hallway. The doors at both ends of it were sealed shut, but another crack in the wall opened into what looked like a rotating wall.

From inside rotating wall, leapt into another gap in the building wall, which brought me to Gear Room.

As I observed the rotating wall, I saw that it had a gap in it. A crazy thought popped into my head: Could I run into that gap the next time it came by? I looked at the DRC safety cones and sawhorse that blocked the entrance to the gap and found myself slightly annoyed by them. That made up my mind. The DRC might not want me doing this, but I wasn't working for them, was I?

I stepped into the gap in the hallway wall and walked right up against the rotating wall, taking care to not get caught in the grooves of what seemed to be teeth wells of an enormous gear. I pressed up against the rotating wall, waiting for the gap to come back around.

A cracked section of the wall preceded the gap by about two seconds. As soon as I saw it, I started running forward and found myself inside the gap of the rotating wall.

Fortunately, the gap was deep enough for me to stand in. If it hadn't been, I realized, I could have wound up crushed between the hallway and the rotating wall by attempting my reckless stunt. I hadn't even considered that. There was something to be said for leaping before you looked.

I stood inside the gap of the rotating wall and observed the building as I moved around it. I saw the gap in the hallway that I'd just run through, but I also saw another gap that led into a room that I hadn't seen yet, a room that was filled with complex machinery.

Once again, I stood at the gap's mouth and pressed up against the wall of the building as I rotated along it. As soon as the gap leading into the new room appeared, I ran through it, again miraculously escaping injury.

Gear Room

The Gear Room. Lots of heavy machinery, with no instruction manual.

Two foot pedals near giant gear.

The room that I'd run into was dominated by a giant gear on the floor, embossed with the crest of the Maintainers (like everything else I'd seen in Gahreesen so far). There were two foot pedals in front of the gear, a bank of five levers on the wall across from the rotating wall, and two doors in the room, both of which were sealed shut.

Bank of five levers.

Two sealed doors.

Third Journey Cloth hung in Gear Room; no more jumping through rotating walls!

THIRD JOURNEY CLOTH

To my delight, I saw the third Journey Cloth hanging on a support pillar to the left of the bank of switches. Now I wouldn't have to pull that crazy run-through-the-gap-in-the-rotating-wall stunt again! I could just link back to this room with the Journey Cloth bookmark in my Gahreesen Linking Book.

PRIMING PUMP

While exploring the Gear Room, I stepped onto a grated platform near the Journey Cloth and almost had a heart attack when some machinery roared into action behind me.

Standing on priming pump pressure plate pressurized pump; stepping off gradually lowered pressure.

After a bit of experimentation, I realized that the platform I stepped onto was the trigger plate for what seemed to be an enormous priming pump. When I stood on it, the pump began to pressurize, and when I stepped off of it, the pressure slowly dropped.

Step 1: Keep priming pump pressurized at all times.

TURNING ON THE POWER

Step 2: Throw leftmost switch. Return to priming pump to repressurize it.

I spent what seemed like the better part of an hour trying to figure out how the switches, foot pedal, and priming pump worked together. Eventually, after a great deal of tedious trial and error, I concluded that they were used in conjunction with each other to supply power to the doors and elevators in the building.

The first step toward restoring the power was to get the large gear in the floor of the Gear Room spinning, which was no easy feat. The gear was secured to the floor with two foot brakes, but to release those brakes, I had to release the primary brake on the gear.

The key to doing all of this was the priming pump. I had to fully prime it and then make sure that it never ran out of pressure; otherwise, I had to start the whole process over again. This meant that I had to perform each step of the process while the pump had pressure and return to the pressure plate after each step to repressurize the pump. Tricky? You bet. But it was obviously not designed to be turned on by one person alone.

I began by priming the pump until it was at full pressure. Then, I <u>ran</u> to the leftmost switch on the row of switches and activated it. As soon as I activated the switch, I ran back to the priming pump and stood on it to pressurize the pump again. As I waited, I saw that the primary brake on the gear had been released.

Step 3: Step on far foot brake from priming pump. Return to pump to repressurize it.

Next, after the pump was fully primed, I ran to the far foot brake and stepped on it, again running back to the priming pump before it lost all of its pressure. I'm reasonably certain that I could have stepped on the near foot brake first, but since it was harder to reach the far brake before the pump ran out of pressure, I decided it would be better to get any failures out of the way early on in the process, thus wasting as little time (and patience) as possible.

Step 4: Step on near foot brake. Return to priming pump to repressurize it.

For the third step, I stood on the priming pump to fully pressurize it. I then ran to the near foot brake, stepped on it to release it, and returned to the priming pump while it still had pressure.

Step 5: Flip second switch from left. Power restored.

When power was restored, the giant gear rose up and meshed into rotating wall grooves.

Finally, after repressurizing the pump one last time, I ran to the second switch from the left (the one with the gear symbol next to it), and I threw the switch. This activated the large gear in the middle of the room. It rose up, and its teeth meshed perfectly into the grooves in the rotating wall, generating power once again.

Once the gear was spinning, I no longer needed to prime the pump. I just flipped the two remaining inactive switches, each of which had elevator symbols next to them. The power was restored.

I flipped the two unlit switches to restore power to the Gahreesen elevators.

The Elevator

With power restored, the Gear Room doors opened for my KI.

Doors at the end of the sections of hallway flashed blue and opened for me.

Once the power was restored, both of the huge stone doors in the Gear Room opened automatically when I approached them. The Maintainer insignia in the center of each door glowed blue as I approached, and I realized that it was my KI that was transmitting the signal to open the doors.

Because both doors led into different ends of the same hall, I realized that it didn't matter which one I went through. The doors at the end of each hallway section opened for me, but the doors on the inside curve of the hall would not open. Instead of a blue insignia, theirs flashed green, implying that they were off-limits to someone who rated only a blue KI. Perhaps the higher-ranking DRC members had more advanced KIs that would open these doors?

Doors on the inner curve of the hallway flashed green and didn't open.

Returned to first floor via the planks over the crumbling wall and floor.

Elevator across from the KI Dispenser room.

After having had my fill of running laps along the halls of the second floor, I decided to return to the first floor and see if turning on the power had opened any new pathways for me down there. I returned to the first floor via the same route I'd used to reach the second floor: through the cracked wall, across the plank, and down into the Beetle Cages.

Just as they did on the second floor, the doors at the end of each of the first floor hallways opened in recognition of my KI, as did the door leading from the hall into the room with the KI Dispenser.

Directly across the hall from the door to the KI Dispenser room was a door with a glowing green light at its center. I pressed the green light and the door opened, revealing an elevator car. I stepped into the elevator, and it went all the way to the top of the building.

Roof

It was the _building_ that was rotating!

Another rotating building? Even bigger, from the look of it.

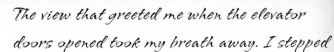

The view that greeted me when the elevator doors opened took my breath away. I stepped out onto the roof of the building, and my first thought was, "How did they get the whole Age to rotate like that?"

It didn't take long for me to realize that it was the <u>building</u> that was rotating. The "rotating wall" that I'd seen on the second floor was actually part of the outdoor landscape, inside of which the entire tower spun. Now the revolving patterns of sunlight in the entrance made sense. Having just come from Teledahn, I'd originally thought that Gahreesen was another Age with a quickly moving sun. Now I realized the sun was stationary; it was the walls that were rotating.

I looked out into the horizon and saw another rotating building adjacent to the one I was on. <u>Two</u> rotating buildings? If there was any doubt in my mind that the D'ni were a society of geniuses, it was put to rest by the sight of those two enormous structures, slowly spinning like two titanic gears.

But why would the Maintainers create rotating buildings? Was it just to show off their skill? No, that wasn't it at all. By building rotating structures, it made it impossible for someone to create a link into any part of them except the dead center, where the Maintainers placed their heavily fortified entrance. If a room's position was constantly changing because it was rotating around an axis, there would be no way to link directly into it unless you linked in at precisely the right time; you'd be just as likely to link outside the building, hundreds of feet in the air—or even into a solid stone wall.

These spinning buildings were the ultimate defense against foes that could link. Maybe the Maintainers had to deal with more internal D'ni conflicts than the history books suggested— or maybe they faced a threat from another race that had mastered the art of linking.

Fourth Journey Cloth

Leaped from first building's pathway to pinnacle between two buildings.

Fourth Journey Cloth hung on the side of the pinnacle.

An extended pathway stretched out from one side of the building's roof. I walked to the edge of it and enjoyed the view, despite the fact that the tremendous height made me a bit queasy.

As the building rotated, I caught sight of a couple of small pinnacles, and one had the fourth Journey Cloth attached to the side of it!

Without pause, I dashed off the end of the walkway and leaped onto the top of the pinnacle with the Journey Cloth. Even though I could have "panic linked" back to Relto had I missed the pinnacle, my heart still thudded in my chest as I touched the Journey Cloth and took a quick breather.

Once my legs stopped shaking, I took a look around at my surroundings. Below the pinnacle on which I stood was a smaller one that overlooked a ledge with the Bahro Cave entrance for Gahreesen. It was good to know where the Bahro Cave door was, but until I had touched all seven Journey Cloths, it wouldn't do me much good.

Bahro Cave entrance below.

Training Facility's pathways rotated past the same pinnacle.

Crazy stunt #2—leaped from pinnacle to Training Facility pathway.

Instead, I turned my attention to the other rotating building (which, I would read in Simpson's journal, was the Maintainers' Training Facility). It dwarfed the size of the first building, which wasn't exactly what you'd call "tiny," either.

Six pathways stretched out from the center of the Training Facility like spokes on an enormous wheel. As the building rotated, the end of each pathway came within a few feet of my current position. Now, I'm not the sort

of person who enjoys death-defying stunts, but I _really_ wanted to see what was in that Training Facility. Plus, until I'd completed Yeesha's journey, I didn't have many other options for returning to the Cleft on earth, so I couldn't afford to leave any areas unexplored.

I squared myself to the Training Facility and waited patiently for one of the pathways to line up with me. As soon as it did, I ran toward it, leaped, and landed on the very edge of the pathway. I couldn't believe I'd done something like that, not just once, but twice! As soon as I could stand again, I ran down the pathway and entered the door to the Training Facility at the end of it.

Training Facility

Simpson mentioned in his journal that this Training Facility was used by the Maintainers to test their environmental variance (EV) suits—used to protect themselves while exploring new Ages— and hone their skills. I would find out later that the upper floors were also used as a maximum-security prison, which further explained the high security for the Age.

The Training Facility had four different types of rooms in it, which Simpson referred to in his journal as Mud Rooms, Control Rooms, Display Rooms, and Conference Rooms.

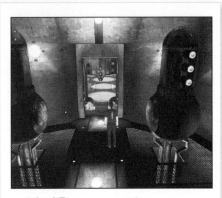

"Mud Room"—another
Gahreesen security feature.

Simpson didn't have a better name for
the rooms beyond each of the six bridges
than "Mud Rooms," named for the
rooms in which houseguests would take
off their muddy shoes. They were the first
rooms that anyone would step into if they
entered the Training Facility via the bridge
(which so far seemed to be the only way to
enter the building).

Simpson guessed that the whole purpose of
the Mud Rooms was to add another layer of
security to the Training Facility. The thick doors between the Mud Rooms and the
Training Facility proper were much more solid than the ones in the first building
and could be sealed securely if the Training Facility were ever attacked.

Beyond the Mud Rooms was a hallway that ran around the entire
circumference of the Training Facility. From that hallway, one could reach the
Control Rooms, Display Rooms, and
Conference Rooms through the doors on the
inside curve of the hallway, or one could leave
the Training Facility via the doors to the Mud
Rooms on the outside curve of the hallway.

Control Room.

CONTROL ROOMS

There were two Control Rooms in the
Training Facility, one for each of the "teams"
of Maintainers that competed against each

other in the Training Room in the center of the facility, which was sort of like the X-Men's Danger Room.

According to Simpson's journal, the Maintainers used these Control Rooms to trigger a variety of extreme environmental conditions in the Training Room, which allowed the Maintainers in to test their skills and equipment.

Although interesting to view, I didn't find anything of importance to my journey in them, though I did notice that a tunnel connected each team's Control Room to its Display Room.

DISPLAY ROOMS

Each of the two Maintainer "teams" had a Display Room in which their suits and other equipment were stored. After getting a good look at some of the equipment in here, I recognized the helmet I saw in Douglas Sharper's Teledahn office as a Maintainer's helmet.

Display Room.

Despite all of the impressive gear on display in these rooms, I found nothing in them that could help me in my journey. Still, it was incredible to see the EV suits up close. It was hard to believe that the Maintainers ever lost a single man with protective equipment like that.

Conference Rooms

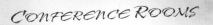

Conference Room.

KI journal, in one
Conference Room.

Simpson's Gahreesen journal,
in the other Conference Room.

There were two of these Conference Rooms, presumably one for each of the Maintainer "teams." They seemed to have been used for observation of the Maintainers in action on the Training Room floor, as well as for meetings and strategy sessions.

I found a DRC notebook with information about the KI in one of the Conference Rooms and Simpson's Gahreesen journal in the other. Both journals were filled with extremely helpful information and were of incalculable value to me in the writing of this journal.

URU
AGES BEYOND MYST.

Prima's Official Travel Guide

EDITOR'S NOTE:
These journals are reprinted in their entirety by kind permission of the DRC in "Appendix B: DRC Research" at the end of this book.

A note about Simpson's journal: On the front of it was a note from Douglas Sharper that read: "Simpson, don't mention anything about the upper area of the fortress in your Gahreesen report. I don't want people wandering all over Teledahn looking for that weird Link Stone." This was my first clue that there was more to Gahreesen than I could reach without using the Linking Stone that I'd found earlier in Teledahn.

Found the fifth Journey Cloth hanging in Conference Room with Simpson's journal.

FIFTH JOURNEY CLOTH

I found the fifth Journey Cloth of Gahreesen hanging on the wall next to the observation window of the Conference Room that also contained Simpson's journal.

After finding the fifth Journey Cloth, I scoured the rest of Gahreesen for the other two, but no matter how many times I retraced my steps, I couldn't find them. It was then that I remembered Sharper's note on Simpson's journal that referred to the Linking Stone in Teledahn. I linked back to Relto in order to return to Teledahn and further investigate that Linking Stone.

Gahreesen Prison
Return to Gahreesen

<u>Teledahn Linking Stone</u>

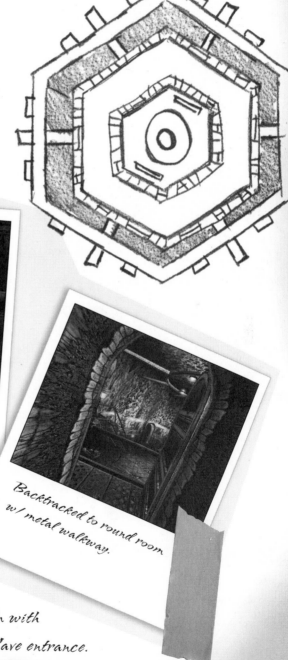

Returned to Teledahn via Journey Cloth bookmark in Linking Book.

Backtracked to round room w/ metal walkway.

After exploring the entire Age and finding only five of Gahreesen's Journey Cloths, I remembered the second Linking Stone in Teledahn, located in the room with the metal walkway near the Bahro Cave entrance.

Because the last Journey Cloth I touched in Teledahn was the one right in front of the Bahro Cave door, I was able to use the Journey Cloth bookmark to link to Teledahn and save a lot of travel.

Linking Stone was still underneath metal walkway, where I'd seen it before.

I ran down the cavern between the Journey Cloth and Bahro Cave door to reach the room with the metal walkway. The Linking Stone was right where I left it. (From what I'd read in Sharper's journal, I don't think I could have moved it from there if I wanted to.)

I placed my hand on the stone's cloth covering and linked to what Simpson's journal referred to as the Gahreesen Prison, located in the same building as the Training Facility.

Another Linking Panel added to the Gahreesen Linking Book after using Linking Stone.

NOTE

When I looked at my Gahreesen Linking Book later, after my journey through the Age was complete, I noticed a second Linking Panel in the Book, behind the main one. It led directly into the Gahreesen Prison; I believe it appeared when I first used the Linking Stone. Had I realized this earlier, I wouldn't have had to go back and find the Teledahn Linking Stone again—I could have linked directly from the Book.

Sixth Journey Cloth and Yeesha Page

Sixth Journey Cloth hung in Gahreesen Prison cell that I linked into.

Yeesha Page found on the prison bed. Added a waterfall to Relto.

I linked directly into a prison cell that had Gahreesen's sixth Journey Cloth hanging on the wall directly in front of me. I touched it. Now there was only one more left to find before I could enter the Bahro Cave.

There wasn't much else to see in the dingy little cell, but I did find another Yeesha Page near the pillow on the bed. When I returned to Relto, I would see that the Yeesha Page had created a waterfall behind my hut.

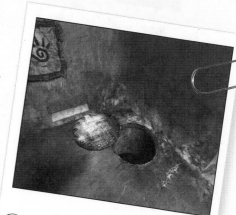

Open hatch in cell floor gave me a way out.

Next to the Journey Cloth was an open hatch in the cell's floor. Grateful for any chance to get out of the claustrophobic chamber, I dropped through it and landed in a corridor below.

I hadn't really considered it before, but the Linking Stone was a highly advanced device. The Gahreesen Prison had been designed to rotate so that no one could use a Linking Book to transport directly into the cells, and yet the Linking Stone seemed to accomplish this feat without any trouble whatsoever. I had seen proof of Yeesha's advanced abilities before, but this was yet another astonishing accomplishment. I wondered where she had learned these skills. Did someone teach her about them? Or did Yeesha have anything to do with these Linking Stones at all?

Seventh Journey Cloth

Walked straight toward a four-way intersection and turned right toward a green light.

At next four-way intersection, I continued going straight.

With my back to the barred window looking outside, I walked forward to a four-way intersection. I turned to my right and walked down the corridor as it curved to the left, illuminated by a green light.

At third four-way intersection, I took a left and climbed the ladder.

At the next four-way intersection, I proceeded straight through, walking toward another green light. At the next four-way intersection, I turned left to see a ladder at the end of the corridor. I reflected back on my short journey through the halls of the prison and realized that I'd traveled counterclockwise through one-quarter of the prison hallway.

Entered large green door in veranda at top of ladder.

Prison Lobby

I walked over to the ladder and climbed it. The ladder led up to the enormous veranda at the top of the Gahreesen Prison. I ran in a counterclockwise direction until I reached a huge green door on the inside curve of the veranda pathway. As I stood in front of the door, it recognized my KI and opened for me.

URU
AGES BEYOND MYST.
Prima's Official Travel Guide

Climbed ladder in the center of the Prison Lobby.

I walked through the door and found myself inside the Prison Lobby. Two ladders stretched up through the roof in the center of the room. Both of them led to the same place—an open-air level of the prison.

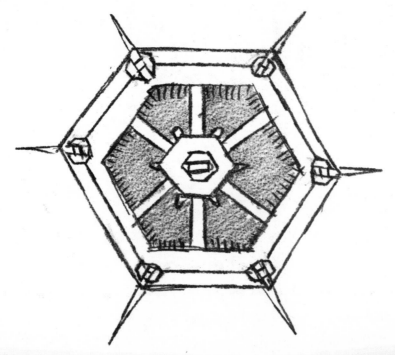

From the top of the ladder, I walked to the edge of the outdoor area.

Walked counterclockwise around the edge until I found the last Journey Cloth.

I ran to the outer ledge of the roof and began walking around it in a counterclockwise direction, the same direction that the building was turning. After a short walk, I saw the seventh and final Journey Cloth hanging on one of the support pillars. I touched it and breathed a sigh of relief as the entire icon lit up. Now I could enter the Bahro Cave.

Had to link back to Relto to leave this part of Gahreesen. Got to admire my new waterfall.

To the Bahro Cave

Linked back to Entrance of Gahreesen and took the elevator to the roof.

Leapt from roof to pinnacle with fourth Journey Cloth. Touched J.C. to activate bookmark in Linking Book in case I screwed up.

In order to leave the Gahreesen Prison, I had to use my Linking Book to return to Relto. From there, I used the Linking Panel in my Gahreesen Linking Book to return to the entrance of the first building (as using the Journey Cloth bookmark would have sent me back to the seventh Journey Cloth in the Training Facility).

From the entrance, I ran in a clockwise direction around the hallway until I reached the elevator. I rode the elevator to the roof of the building and walked to the edge of the extended pathway, waiting for the tall pinnacle that stood between the two buildings to come into range.

Once it did, I leapt to it with a running jump and immediately stopped my forward momentum so that I didn't run right off the edge.

I was really starting to lose my nerve when it came to these jumps, so I touched the nearby Journey Cloth to provide a quick link back here, and then I turned in the direction of the Bahro Cave door. Directly in front of me was a lower pinnacle that overlooked the Cave door.

Leapt from Journey Cloth pinnacle to lower pinnacle in front of me.

I crossed my fingers, made sure my Linking Book was at the ready, and hopped to the pinnacle. From there, I made one of the longest and most nerve-wracking leaps of my life, landing safely on the ledge with the Bahro Cave door on it. I placed my sweating palm on the door's hand imprint, and like the one in Teledahn, it slid open and admitted me to the pitch-black cavern inside.

Made huge jump from lower pinnacle to ledge w/ Bahro Cave door on it.

Bahro Cave door opened when I touched the hand icon.

I stepped into the cavern and heard the same squeaking and flapping of giant wings that I'd heard in the Teledahn cavern. So those giant bats lived on Gahreesen as well, eh? Great. I walked forward as quickly as I could until I felt myself link away from the unsettling noises that echoed in the inky blackness of the cavern.

Bahro Cave

I materialized inside of the Bahro Cave, which at first glance appeared to be the same cave I'd visited at the end of my Teledahn journey. On closer inspection, however, I realized that that couldn't possibly have been the case.

When I linked into the cave at the end of Teledahn, the rocky ledge that I appeared on was obviously larger than the other three ledges, and it was the only ledge with a symbol etched into its floor.

Could this be the same Bahro Cave I entered from Teledahn? Don't think so.

The ledge I stood on here still had its Bahro Pillar, and it also had a symbol etched into its floor, but it was a different symbol than I'd seen previously. The ledge was also clearly larger than the other three, one of which was missing its Bahro Pillar. How was that possible? Was I linking into different caves from each Age? Were they somehow related so that a change in one was reflected in the others?

Yeesha's disembodied voice distracted me from pondering the matter further and drew my undivided attention. I recorded her words for transcription later:

"Sho-rah. Peace to you, mover of the Least. Seven more Journeys have moved you closer.

"I was seduced while in D'ni. My humble darkness lasted only a short time, before I began to bask in what I could do—what I could write. My gift, my path, the knowledge of my father, and the dreams of my mother, pierced a hole in the darkness, in the weakness. I was aware of my power, and I was proud . . . whole worlds at my fingertips.

"It was the same with the D'ni, the same cycle.

"Light opens the darkness. It takes, it uses, and it keeps. The D'ni found power in these books. These books you use to travel, they were a gift from the Maker. These Ages you travel to were their Ages—remarkable places, giving life . . . and taking life.

"This shadow came over them, this shadow of light. For it was in their enlightenment that they considered themselves better . . . better than the Least.

"And we were sad for them.

"Can you feel the D'ni there? You've touched the remnants—the remains of their pride and power.

"Let me tell you of King Kerath, dare I speak ill of him. One of the great kings, but yet he was the maker of the proud. For it was his system of Guilds that served as the foundation of power . . . and corruption.

"The powerful need control, fortresses and garrisons to guard their power. And soon the guarding is yet another thing to be proud of.

"Layers within layers built to preserve their Ages and their pride from the weak and Least who might attack from without. And yet it is from within that most nations fall, and so the mighty garrisons of D'ni now stand vacant.

"The writing hides what's between the lines. These journeys are to help you travel between.

"The Bahro will be returned. These Pillars are our journey. The return of the Pillars is the return of the Bahro. The bringing away and the bringing back."

More Questions, More Answers

Yeesha's words cleared up a few questions for me, but they left me with a few new ones as well. She spoke of being overcome with pride while studying the Art of Writing in D'ni. If I understood her correctly, there came a point at which she realized that D'ni was not as pure and wholesome as she'd been led to believe, that aspects of the society were in some way oppressive to the people she called "the Least."

I was relatively certain by this point that "the Least" were a specific class or race of beings, and that the Bahro either were the Least or were part of a more general group that composed the Least. I assumed that the Least were not D'ni, judging from the way that the Maintainers had apparently imprisoned them in Gahreesen and Manesmo was able to get away with enslaving them in Teledahn. Yeesha had also referred to the D'ni view of the Least in her Teledahn speech as "animals that could link."

Were these the same "Bahro" referred to in _The Book of D'ni_, the "unseen" _relyimah_ forced into slavery by the people of Terahnee? It seemed unlikely. When Atrus first encountered the _relyimah_ in Terahnee, he was completely unfamiliar with the race or the custom of slavery, and the _relyimah_ knew nothing of D'ni. Had the _relyimah_ been brought to D'ni at some point in the past, Atrus would have been familiar with the race, or the _relyimah_ would have been familiar with the D'ni.

Furthermore, according to *The Book of Ti'ana*, when Anna first arrived in D'ni from the surface of the earth, she was considered to be an unthinking brute, little more than a beast. There was a debate among the D'ni as to whether she should be expelled from the city or kept there, but there was no question of enslaving her or denying her basic rights that the D'ni seemed to guarantee to all sentient creatures.

No, according to *The Book of D'ni*, "bahro" was derived from the D'ni word "bah," which meant "beast." It was more likely that "bahro" was the D'ni word that most closely approximated "least," in the context of discussing living beings.

Yeesha's reference to "fortresses and garrisons" was obviously a statement about the Gahreesen Age. Although she dismisses the constructs as foolish attempts to defend the D'ni from external threats, the very fact that they were developed meant that the D'ni must have felt some sort of threat, either from the Bahro or from someone else. And yet, while the prison was huge, it didn't seem large enough to imprison more than a hundred or so prisoners at most.

Still, maybe there were hundreds of Ages similar to Gahreesen. Maybe the Maintainers spread out their prisoners across many Ages to prevent any chance of a mass jailbreak. In that case, the D'ni could have had thousands or millions of Bahro prisoners, and Yeesha's description of the D'ni obsession with fortifications would have made sense—in fact, it would be hard to imagine the Bahro not attacking D'ni in that situation. Whatever menace the Bahro represented to D'ni, however, they weren't the cause of the city's downfall. That came when the disgraced D'ni guildsmen known as Veovis and A'Geris unleashed the plague that destroyed D'ni more than 200 years ago.

I didn't know what Yeesha meant when she said that "the writing hides what's between the lines." By "writing," did she mean the journals that were kept by her mother, on which *The Book of Atrus*, *The Book of Ti'ana*, and *The Book of D'ni*

were based? Or did she mean "writing" in the larger sense of the volumes of D'ni history that the DRC were only just beginning to discover and translate.

Or, did I perhaps miss a capital "W" in her speech? Was she trying to say that the glorious D'ni Art of "Writing," which created links to worlds of infinite possibilities, were not always used for the noble and scholarly purposes that the D'ni claimed they were? It was a question that only Yeesha could answer, and because I'd only heard recordings of her monologues, I was left with only guesses and speculation.

Yeesha's last lines shed a bit more light on the purpose of my journey. If the Bahro Pillars were "the very being of the Bahro," as she said after my Teledahn journey, then perhaps by removing the Pillars from their D'ni-written Ages, I was somehow rescuing the Bahro from some form of imprisonment. But I still didn't know what Yeesha's line about "the bringing away and the bringing back" meant. Maybe by "bringing away" the Pillars to Relto, I was "bringing back" the Bahro? The Pillars didn't seem to do anything in Relto, but perhaps that was because I hadn't retrieved all four of them yet.

Return to Relto

Despite the fact that I still didn't have a clear idea of exactly what I was doing or why I was doing it, I felt like I was getting closer to understanding the point of the journey Yeesha asked me to undertake. And though my path

Touched hand icon on the wall to remove Bahro Pillar to Relto.

still wasn't as clear as it could have been, I still had two more Ages to
explore: Kadish Tolesa and the paired Ages of Eder Gira and Eder Kemo.
That meant that I'd probably hear two more of Yeesha's speeches, which
might help to clarify matters more.

Leapt into starry void to link
back to Relto.

Bahro Pillar reappeared on
pedestal in Relto.

In any event, there was
nothing more for me to do in this
cave. Just as I'd done in the Bahro Cave at the end of Teledahn, I touched the
hand print icon on the wall to remove the Bahro Pillar from the stone ledge,
and then I walked off of the ledge and fell into the starry void below.

I reappeared in Relto, less shaken than I was after my previous
experience falling into the starry void, but still more than a bit rattled. There
had to be an easier way for Yeesha to get me out of that cave! Or those
caves. Or whatever.

As before, the Bahro Pillar came with me and materialized on top of its
Age's pedestal, and the pedestal sunk into the ground. Two Bahro Pillars
found. Two left to go. After a bit of rest and freshening up, I would make
the link to Kadish Tolesa and see if I could find the third Pillar.

Kadish Tolesa

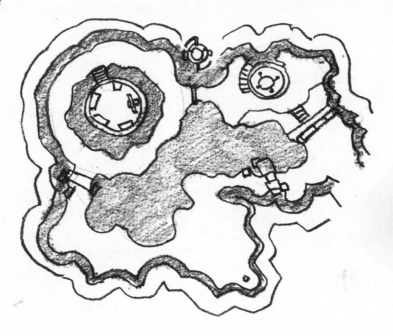

Kadish Tolesa pedestal was the far right one from the hut.

Image on top of pedestal seemed to be a stylized tree.

As I stood with my back to Relto's hut, the Linking Book to Kadish Tolesa was located in the far right pedestal. As with the other pedestals, I just had to place my hand on the pedestal to access the Linking Book.

The Book's Linking Panel showed an image of what appeared to be the base of an enormous tree, a hypothesis confirmed by the symbol on top of the pedestal, which looked like an abstract, stylized tree. I placed my hand on the Linking Panel and slipped through the link to Kadish Tolesa. (When I returned to Relto later, I would find the Kadish Tolesa Linking Book on my Library shelf in the third slot from the left.)

The Forest

I linked to the base of the largest tree I'd ever seen.

Took the path to the left of the tree (as I faced the tree).

Upon linking to Kadish Tolesa, I turned around and looked up. Sure enough, I had arrived in a forest of the largest trees I'd ever seen. I couldn't crane my neck back far enough to see the tops of the trees without falling over. Fragments of giant stone arches clung to the trunks, but compared to the trees, the arches looked like remnants of a toy castle.

As I faced the huge tree and stone arches before me, I saw that there were two paths I could follow: one to the right and one to the left. I chose the left path and started walking.

The forest path led to a ruined courtyard, the floor of which had collapsed into a yawning chasm below. In the center of the chasm was another titanic tree that had been hollowed out and lined with once-beautiful arches. Before it fell to ruin, it was probably the most impressive gazebo ever built. As I looked at the crumbling masonry, I wondered (as I had in Gahreesen) if the destruction was the result of a natural phenomenon or if some incredible force had visited the destruction upon the Age.

FIRST JOURNEY CLOTH

Path ended in a ruined courtyard, with a gazebo in the center.

Walked all the way around the perimeter of the courtyard and found the first Journey Cloth.

Before climbing the stone stairs to the elevated platform in the center of the courtyard, I examined the remains of the courtyard. I was rewarded for my curiosity. As I walked in a clockwise circle along the courtyard's outer edge, I found the Age's first Journey Cloth hanging on the back of one of the support pillars.

Kadish Tolesa Gallery

On one side of the gazebo was a strange telescopic device.

On the other side of the gazebo was a Linking Book to a Gallery in the D'ni city.

After touching the first Journey Cloth and exploring the courtyard to my satisfaction, I backtracked to the large set of stairs that led to the gazebo in the center of the courtyard and climbed them.

On one side of the gazebo was some sort of telescopic device with a three-ringed apparatus beyond it. I took a quick peek through the viewfinder and saw a magnified image of the three concentric rings along with buttons for

Linking Book had the DRC seal of approval—figured it was safe to use.

rotating them. I knew a puzzle when I saw one, and because I had no clue how to solve it at the moment, I turned my attention to the other side of the gazebo, where I found a Linking Book.

URU
AGES BEYOND MYST.
Prima's Official Travel Guide

The Linking Book was stamped with a DRC symbol, so I figured that it must be safe to link through. Placing my hand on the Linking Panel, I disappeared from Kadish Tolesa and reappeared in some sort of art gallery.

A Linking Book sat on a pedestal in the center of the Gallery, with an image of the forest gazebo on its linking panel, obviously designed for Gallery visitors to return to the place from which they had linked.

Artwork #1: Stained-glass triptych.

Artwork #2: Blue stained-glass panel.

Artwork #3: Rotating triangular blocks on pillars.

Five works of art were displayed prominently around the Linking Book. The first one I looked at was a triptych of three round stained glass patterns. They looked somewhat like the concentric rings I'd seen through the viewfinder of that device on the Kadish Tolesa gazebo. Leave it to the D'ni to create beautiful works of art that were practical clues at the same time.

I took several photographs of the triptych, and then I photographed the other artworks, just in case they were clues for other puzzles later on. (It was one of the best decisions I made during my entire journey, because it turned out that I was exactly right.)

Next to the triptych was another round piece of stained glass. The blue light that shone through it illuminated a crookedly curving pattern through its center. On closer inspection, I also saw five blue circles on the outer edge of the left side of the design. Three of them were much brighter than the other two.

Moving counterclockwise around the room, the next piece of art on display was a series of six small pillars, each of which was numbered (from left to right) 1-6 in D'ni characters. Atop each pillar was a rotating golden triangular block, and on each side of each block was a variation on a similar pattern. I photographed all three patterns for each block.

Artwork #4: Stained-glass panel w/ rotating perimeter. A clock?

Artwork #5: Stained-glass panel w/ abstract designs on it.

Next to the rotating triangular block artwork was another stained-glass pattern. In its center were four vertical lines, one red, one white, one green, and one blue. The D'ni symbols for the numerals 1-4 lined the rotating perimeter of the pattern. Was this some kind of clock? I noticed that three of the

numerals on the perimeter were red, three were white, three were green, and three were blue, but I didn't know what to make of it, so I moved on.

The final piece of artwork on display was another stained-glass panel, but it was much too abstract for me to make any sense out of. At the top was the tree motif that I'd seen on the Kadish Tolesa pedestal in Relto; it was also repeated many times in this Gallery. There were three white circles in the middle of the design, and a white triangle was overlaid on the center circle. A smaller circle with concentric rings inside of it sat atop the triangle.

Couldn't move past the DRC sawhorses.

Linking Book transported me back to courtyard gazebo in Kadish Tolesa.

A pair of sweeping staircases at one end of the Gallery led to two DRC sawhorses, preventing me from leaving except via the Linking Book. I was slightly annoyed at that, because I was sure that the Linking Book I'd used was a traditional D'ni Linking Book, which meant that I had linked from Kadish Tolesa to another Age, possibly even D'ni again. I would have loved to investigate it further, but the DRC were apparently keeping the rest of this Age to themselves for the time being. Oh well.

I'd seen just about all there was to see in the Gallery, and I'd photographed just about every square inch of it, so I felt confident that if these artworks were clues for upcoming puzzles (as the triptych seemed to be), I'd have easy access to all of the information I needed to solve them.

Stepping onto the raised platform in the center of the Gallery, I placed my hand on the Linking Book and returned to Kadish Tolesa.

Triptych Design Alignment

FIRST DESIGN

I looked through the viewfinder of the device on the gazebo. Sure enough, the pattern I saw definitely resembled the designs of the stained glass triptych I'd seen in the Gallery.

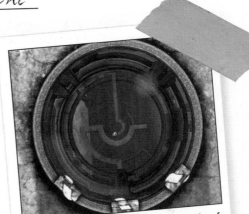

The proper alignment for the first design. Left button: all 3 rings. Middle button: tan & lt. brown rings. Right button: lt. brown ring.

There were three buttons along the viewfinder's bottom. The left one turned all three of the patterns—tan, light brown, and dark brown—45 degrees counterclockwise. The middle one moved only the tan and light brown patterns, and the right one moved only the light brown one.

Because it was the only button that could move the dark brown pattern, I used the left one to align the dark brown pattern according to the top design of the Gallery triptych. I then used the middle button to line up the tan pattern. Finally, I used the right button to put the light brown pattern in its proper position.

When I finished, I took a photo through the viewfinder lens and compared it to the top image from the Gallery triptych; they matched perfectly. I was definitely on to something.

SECOND DESIGN

Passed through round archway.

Returned to link-in point, took the right-hand path (as I faced the giant tree.

I left the gazebo in search of the next ringed design. I saw another viewing device in the distance, past the one I'd just used, but there was no way to get there directly.

Turned left at fork, went under ring design.

I headed down the stairs back to the courtyard and retraced my steps to my link-in position. This time, I took the right-hand path (as I stood facing the giant tree and stone arches). This brought me to the ruins of a round archway, which I passed through. At a fork in the path, I turned left to see another ring design and, on a raised platform beyond it, an alignment device.

Alignment device for the second design was on top of a raised platform.

Proper alignment for the second design. Same controls as first.

I walked around the left side of the platform to find a set of stairs leading up to the alignment device. This alignment device was a bit more confusing, because the design from the first device was superimposed on the design for this one. I had to mentally block out the first device's design in order to focus on the one I had to align here.

Once again, there were three buttons on the viewer. The left one moved all three patterns of the design: tan, light brown, and dark brown. The middle one moved only the tan and light brown patterns. The right one controlled only the light brown pattern.

Using the left button to align the dark brown pattern, the middle one to align the tan pattern, and the right one to align the light brown pattern, I wound up with a design that looked like the second panel of the Gallery triptych. I compared the photo I took of the finished design to the photo of the second panel of the Gallery triptych, and they matched perfectly. Two down, one to go.

SECOND JOURNEY CLOTH

After aligning the second ring design, I walked around the base of the platform that the alignment device sat on. Hanging on the side of the platform was the second Journey Cloth. I touched it to activate it.

Second J.C. was on the side of the alignment device platform.

Linking Stone

Found a Linking Stone near the stairs to the platform with the alignment device on it.

Before I left in search of the third alignment device, I further explored the immediate area. I'd nearly walked past the second Journey Cloth without seeing it, and I didn't want to run the risk of missing anything else of importance.

Linking Stone brought me to another balcony overlooking the D'ni city.

Had to link back to Relto to leave the balcony. Kadish Tolesa Linking Book was third from the left in the Library.

It's a good thing that I decided to hang around, because near the stairs of the platform was another Linking Stone. Because I'd just touched the second Journey Cloth, I realized that I could return to this exact position quickly and easily from the Linking Book on Relto. I placed my hand on the cloth-covered linking panel and felt myself pulled into the eerie coolness.

I reappeared on another balcony overlooking the city of D'ni. Looking over the railing, I saw the lights of DRC sawhorses lining a ledge that overlooked a sheer drop into a canyon below. As I gazed out at the doorways to D'ni houses, I felt another pang of regret at blowing off the DRC so quickly. They might be a little too bureaucratic, and they might suffer from a lack of imagination, but they got to walk the streets of D'ni itself, while I could only gaze at it from afar.

The door that led out onto the balcony was sealed shut and wouldn't budge. Once again, the only option for me was to use my Linking Book to return to Relto and link back to Kadish Tolesa from the Book in my Library.

As I returned to Kadish Tolesa, I thought some more about the Linking Stones that I'd used. They had properties that D'ni Linking Books didn't share (such as the ability to link into the rotating prison in Gahreesen). The cloth that covered them resembled the Journey Cloths that served as markers of the history of the Bahro. Did the Bahro make the Linking Stones? It was certainly a question worth pondering, but the odds of me getting an answer without speaking to Yeesha or the Bahro themselves were slim.

Third Design

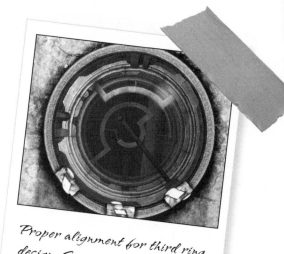

Proper alignment for third ring design. Same controls as first and second.

Backtracked away from second alignment device and headed straight forward to see third device.

Upon linking back to Kadish Tolesa's second Journey Cloth, I headed back down the pathway that ran under the second ring design. There was something just past it, a little farther down the path. I ran to it and found the third alignment device aimed at the third ring design.

Looking through the alignment device, I found that the controls were exactly the same as the first two. The left button rotated the gray, light brown, and dark brown patterns. The middle button rotated the gray and light brown patterns. And the right button rotated only the light brown pattern.

Aligning all three patterns correctly opened a doorway in the tree beyond the third design.

I used the left button to set the dark brown pattern, the middle button to set the gray pattern, and the right button to set the light brown pattern. As soon as I aligned the final pattern correctly, I saw something in the background of the viewfinder slide to the left. Looking away from the viewfinder, I saw that a door had opened inside of a tree just past the third ring pattern. Bingo.

I set up my camera to take a picture of the viewfinder, just in case I made a mistake later on in my journey and had to erase this instance of the Age. Once I had the photo, I entered the tree.

Third Journey Cloth

On the other side of the small anteroom beyond the tree door was a blue button on the wall. I pressed it, and the entire anteroom turned a few feet counterclockwise, resetting the door to its closed position.

Pressing this button closed the doorway I just opened.

Third Journey Cloth was on the back of the door; revealed when I closed the door.

I stepped back into the anteroom and saw the third Journey Cloth hanging in the now-closed doorway that previously led outside. I touched the Cloth, grateful for the very necessary shortcut back to this area now that the door was closed.

Shadow Path

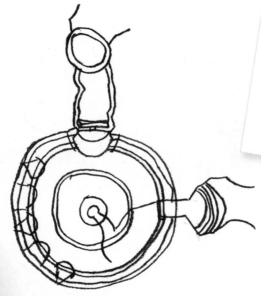

Spiraling pathway led down to the floor past five glowing blue switches.

I proceeded down the cracked stone path and into the room beyond it, a tall cylindrical space with a translucent blue crystal in the roof that filtered a soft

Blue stained-glass artwork in Gallery was the clue—dots in upper-left corner represented five switches.

light to the floor. Just below the blue crystal hung what looked like a mobile of large curved pieces of stone.

A stone walkway spiraled down along the inside of the wall and down to the floor. Near the end of the walkway were five glowing blue switches along its inside curve.

The floor was made of stone, with curving lines and circles etched into it. At one end of the floor was a locked door that resisted my best attempts to open it. Another puzzle.

I pulled out my photographs of the Gallery artwork, and the round blue stained-glass panel caught my eye. It was the same color as the blue crystal in the ceiling of this room, and the lines running through its center resembled the curving lines of the floor. But what was the secret?

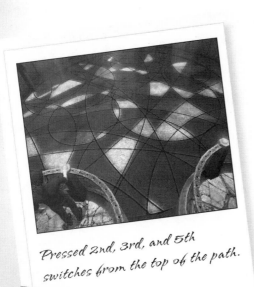

Pressed 2nd, 3rd, and 5th switches from the top of the path.

Walked along _shadow_ path, not light path, into center of floor.

It was then that I remembered the five buttons on the left side of the stained-glass panel. The second, third, and fifth ones were lit; the first and fourth were dimmed. I realized that those must have been intended to represent the blue switches on the walkway.

Floor sunk to become stairs that led to a hidden door.

I headed back up the walkway, past the switches, and then I turned around and walked toward them, ignoring the first switch, turning on the second and third, skipping the fourth, and turning on the fifth.

Each switch that I turned on illuminated some of the floor, forming a pathway of light along the floor of the room. The foot of the stairs was directly across from the sealed door, so I reasoned that crossing the lit path from the stairs to the door was the key to opening it. No such luck. Repeated attempts to open the door proved futile.

I sat down at the foot of the steps and consulted my notes. In the Relto book that referred to the various Ages, Yeesha chose a quote for Kadish Tolesa that ended with, "Look deep, ponder and recognize all that is hidden." That had to be some sort of clue.

I looked at the floor again and noticed a shadowy path leading to the center of the room. Envisioning the floor as the face of a clock, the sealed door would be at the 12 o'clock position, the foot of the stairs would be 6 o'clock, and the start of the shadow path would be around 2 o'clock. I made my way around the edge of the floor and began walking along the shadow path to the room's center, careful to avoid stepping in any illuminated areas of the floor.

As soon as I reached the center of the floor, the sections of the shadow path sunk and transformed into a set of stairs that led down to a secret door!

I headed down the newly formed staircase and through the doorway at its bottom.

This switch on the other side of the door reset the shadow path puzzle.

A set of amphitheater stairs led up from the other side of the door, and at the top was another blue crystal switch. I pressed the switch and heard the sections of floor that made the shadow path rise up to their original positions, sealing me in this new area of Kadish Tolesa. It was time to find another Journey Cloth, just in case I had to leave the Age; I didn't want to mess with the shadow path again.

Yeesha Page and Fourth Journey Cloth

Path led to a foggy waterfront—beautiful and creepy.

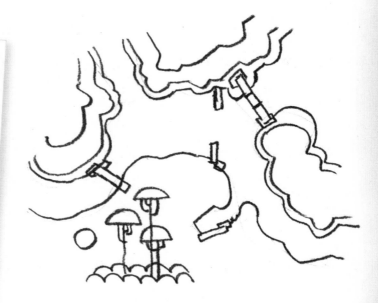

Thought there might be something on the other side of this gap . . .

. . . and I was right—another Yeesha Page!

I walked along the stone pathway past more ruined arches until it opened into a breathtaking misty waterfront vista. Tall, slender trees with tiny tufts of leaves atop them rose eerily up from the fog. The path ended in an abrupt ledge over the water and curved to the left, up to a set of stairs.

To the right of the stairs, the ledge was split in two by an enormous crack. There didn't seem to be much of interest on the other side of the gap, but I had learned that things weren't often what they seemed to be in Kadish Tolesa. I walked to the edge of the ledge, backed up a few steps, and then ran and leaped over it to the other side.

My instincts turned out to be worth following. There, lying on the gap's other side, was another Yeesha Page. I picked it up and touched its design—the image of a sapling tree—before adding it to my Linking Book. (When I returned to Relto, I would see that the Page had added small growing pine trees to the island.)

Ziggurat was an amazing thing to see in person. Wondered what was around the side of it?

Saw the fourth Journey Cloth in an alcove on the outside of the ziggurat.

After satisfying myself that there was nothing else of interest on this side of the ledge, I jumped back over the gap and proceeded up the stone stairs into a tall cavern with an immense ziggurat in its middle. The front door of the ziggurat was open, but I wanted to examine its exterior first.

Once again, my developing sense of curiosity paid off. As I ran in a clockwise direction around the structure, I saw the fourth Journey Cloth in an exterior alcove of the ziggurat. Touching it not only moved me one step closer to completing my journey through the Age, but it also updated my Kadish Tolesa Linking Book bookmark, allowing me to link directly back here if necessary.

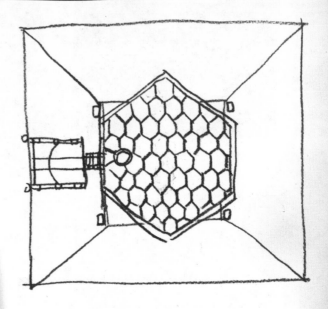

The floor of the ziggurat was covered with hexagonal tiles w/ symbols on them.

Blue crystal switch shone light into the room.

This artwork was the clue, but what did it mean?

After activating the Journey Cloth, I entered the ziggurat. From the entrance, I could go straight ahead and up a few stairs to a control panel with a single blue crystal switch, or I could walk directly out onto the floor of the room.

The floor was covered with hexagonal tiles, each of which bore the faint image of a rune. I had seen many of the runes on the rotating triangular blocks in the Gallery. The perimeter of the room was lined with ten sealed doors.

I pressed the glowing blue crystal, and a giant sphere in the ceiling rotated and shone a brilliant light down into the room. At least now I had a better view of what I was doing.

I flipped through my photos of the three remaining Gallery artwork clues. Although, some of the symbols on the floor matched those on the rotating triangular blocks, I didn't see any connection between the artwork and this puzzle; I had the feeling that those symbols were most likely just generic D'ni symbols (or at least symbols common to Kadish Tolesa). The rotating stained-glass design with the red, white, blue, and green numbers around the edge didn't seem to apply here either.

Pressing the blue switch again shut off the light. Floor tiles glowed with different symbols.

Key to making it across the floor was to only step on tiles with "tree-shaped" symbols.

The only artwork clue left was the abstract array of stained-glass shapes. I studied it for several minutes but was unable to make any sense out of that one either. Frustrated, I hit the blue switch again, and the hexagonal floor tiles glowed with a faint blue light, displaying different symbols than they had previously.

I looked at the photo of the abstract piece of art again. Now it was starting to make a bit more sense. The triangle in th middle represented either the ziggurat or the light from the ceiling, and the concentric circles at the top of it were meant to indicate the sphere that shone the light into the room.

Having just walked the shadow path, I guessed that this was another "path" puzzle. I looked at the photo again and saw the abstract treelike symbol at the top of it, the same symbol that had been repeated often throughout the Gallery and in the objects and documents associated with Kadish Tolesa.

Tree shape, variation #1.

Tree shape, variation #2.

Tree shape, variation #3.

Tree shape, variation #4.

As I looked out over the floor, I noted with some excitement that it was possible to start walking from the right side of the floor entrance, all the way across to a door in the far wall by stepping only on tiles that glowed with the four variations of the tree symbol. The key was to look for symbols with a rounded top and three "branches" extending below it that joined to form the trunk of the tree.

I walked from tile to tile with extreme care. When I reached the end of the path, on the tenth tile, I stood and waited for something to happen, for one of the doors to open, for anything at all.

I had just about given up when the tile on which I stood shuddered and descended into the floor. It was a hidden elevator! Kadish Tolesa's <u>Indiana Jones</u>-style puzzles were obviously designed to hide someone or something—was this more of the D'ni paranoia that Yeesha saw reflected in the fortresses and garrisons of Gahreesen?

After walking the path, the last tile sunk into the ground— an elevator!

Fifth Journey Cloth

Prima's Official Travel Guide

The floor-tile elevator brought me down to another cavern, and I saw the fifth Journey Cloth of Kadish Tolesa hanging on the cavern wall in front of me. I stepped off of the floor tile, and it rose back up into the ceiling. For a moment, I thought I had lost the use of it, but then it descended again.

Fifth Journey Cloth hung on the wall just beyond the glowing pathway elevator.

I touched the Journey Cloth to activate it, and then I returned to a glowing blue switch I'd seen near the elevator. I pressed it, and the elevator reset itself. Unless I linked out of here, there was nowhere to go but forward.

The Pillars

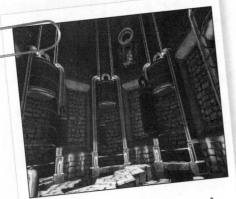

Next room had four levers and four large hexagonal tiles (tops of pillars).

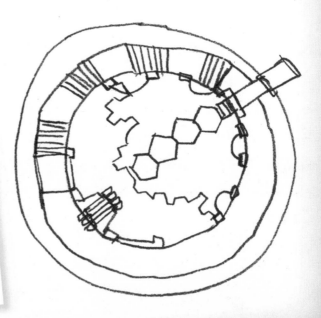

Left lever raised nearest pillar, lever second from the left raised next-closest pillar, etc. Blue switch reset them.

To reach alcove above the other side of the room, I raised 2nd pillar 1x, 3rd pillar 3x, 4th pillar 4x.

The next cylindrical room was so tall that the top of it was lost to darkness. An elaborate system of pulleys and counterweights hung from above, and a bridge of four hexagonal floor tiles stretched to the other side of the room across a gaping chasm.

At the end of the hexagonal floor tiles were four levers and a blue switch. I pulled the leftmost lever, and the hexagonal floor tile directly in front of me rose about 20 or 30 feet into the air, revealing a ladder on its near side. I pulled the lever again, and the pillar rose even higher. I pulled the rightmost lever, and the farthest tile rose into the air. Pressing the blue switch returned the pillars to floor level.

After a bit of experimentation, I realized that the levers, from left to right, controlled the elevation of the pillars, from nearest to farthest. The blue switch was the reset switch. I also learned that I could raise the pillars a total of only eight times before the mechanism ran out of counterweight and could no longer be operated.

I saw that there was an alcove high above the floor on the far side of the room. The pillars seemed to be designed to reach it. What a simple puzzle; I didn't even need the Gallery clue to solve it!

To reach the alcove, I pulled the fourth (rightmost) handle a total of four times, the third (second from right) handle three times, and the second (from left) handle once. I was then able to climb up the pillars' ladders and reach the alcove with ease.

Sixth Journey Cloth

Found the sixth Journey Cloth inside of the alcove.

A set of stairs led back down to the floor with the pillar levers.

The sixth Journey Cloth hung inside of the alcove. I strode confidently into the alcove and touched it. To the left of a Journey Cloth was a spiraling staircase leading down. That was the only way to go, so I hopped down the stairs with a spring in my step, ready for the next puzzle.

The stairs ended at a sealed door with a lever in front of it. I lifted the lever, and the door opened, revealing the ground floor of the pillar puzzle. The blood drained out of my face, and my cockiness drained with it. Sighing, I sat down and pulled out my Gallery photographs.

The "clock" stained-glass artwork was the key to the solution.

Had to reset pillars, then raise 1st pillar 1x, 2nd pillar 4x, 3rd pillar 1x, and 4th pillar 2x. Ladder fell from ceiling to 2nd pillar.

Climbed ladder to reach the next puzzle.

There were only two Gallery artwork clues that I hadn't used: the rotating triangular blocks, and the clocklike stained-glass window. I realized almost immediately that the "clock" artwork had to be the key, because the red, white, green, and blue designs in the center of it looked like they were meant to represent the pillars.

I then took a look at the D'ni numerical symbols on the outer edge of the design. Each color (red, white, green, and blue) appeared as the background color for three numerals:

Red: 2, 3, 4	Green: 2, 3, 4
White: 1, 2, 3	Blue: 1, 3, 4

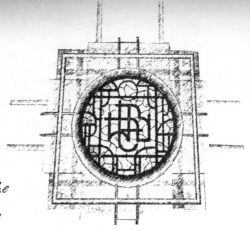

After looking at my notes, I thought I had the answer: I needed to raise each pillar the number of times that was _missing_ from the series of numbers. So if the red pillar was the first one (controlled by the left lever), I had to raise it one step, then the second pillar four steps, the third pillar one step, and the fourth (right lever) two steps.

I pressed the blue button to reset the pillars, and then I raised each pillar by the number of steps that I'd just calculated.

As soon as all four pillars were in the 1-4-1-2 pattern, I saw a series of large concentric stone circles drop from the ceiling right above the top of the elevated second pillar. A ladder descended from them, coming to rest just above the top of the pillar. Success!

I climbed to the very top of the second pillar, where I got a better view of the ladder. The extremely long ladder. From where I was standing, it seemed as if the top of it must have been at least at the level of the glowing symbols floor of the ziggurat, if not higher.

I started to climb, and as I did, I reflected back on my overconfidence at the start of the pillar puzzle. Although I felt foolish about thinking that I'd solved the puzzle right off the bat, I also realized that solving the puzzle correctly on the first try would have kept me from getting the sixth Journey Cloth. That made me feel a bit better, but I resolved to try and retain a bit more humility in the future. _After all_, I thought as I looked down into the inky blackness far below me, _pride goes before a fall._

The Vault

The final puzzle: a cube-shaped vault suspended by guy wires the size of oil pipelines.

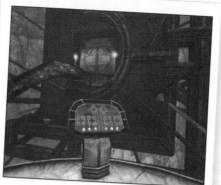

A control panel in front of the vault was where the combination had to be entered.

At the top of the ladder was a wide stone cavern. A blue crystal switch on the right side of the cavern wall reset the pillars to their original position. I walked down to the end of the cavern, where I saw yet another stunning example of D'ni ingenuity.

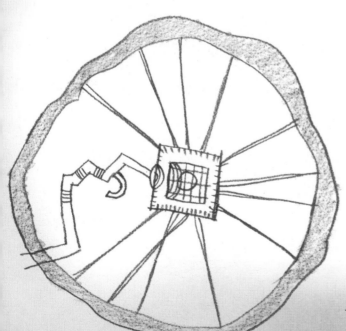

Inside the largest vertical cavern I'd ever seen, a cube-shaped vault was suspended by dozens of guy wires large enough to walk across. I couldn't tell if the cavern was made of stone or if it was constructed inside of a tree so old and so enormous that the wood had petrified, but there was no doubt that no one was going to reach this place unless they managed to solve the puzzles that guarded it.

And now one final puzzle remained. On the pathway leading up to the vault entrance was a control console. Six buttons were along the bottom of it, and from each button was drawn a line that ended a symbol. I looked at my photographs, realizing that the rotating triangular block artwork must be the clue for this final puzzle.

1st set of rotating block symbols.

2nd set of rotating block symbols.

3rd set of rotating block symbols.

The six buttons obviously corresponded to the six pillars. And each of the six buttons had four symbols associated with it. I made a leap of logic and guessed that the pillars, numbered 1–6, somehow represented the order in which the buttons should be pressed.

I looked at the symbols on the Gallery pillars and compared them to the symbols associated with each button. Drawing on my experience with the pillar puzzle, I made a list of which buttons were <u>not</u> associated with which pillars (because they were <u>not</u> labeled with symbols from the pillar).

Vault Combination, Step One

Button	Pillar (Order)
1st	1st, 5th
2nd	1st, 2nd, 3rd
3rd	1st, 3rd, 4th
4th	4th, 5th
5th	2nd
6th	1st, 6th

I assumed that the first button was to be the first button pressed in the combination (because it was labeled with a D'ni "1"), then I could eliminate all of the "1sts" from the order column, because I'd already decided which button was going to be pressed first; it was now just a matter of determining the order of the 2nd through 6th buttons:

Vault Combination, Step Two

Button	Pillar (Order)
1st	1st (confirmed)
2nd	2nd, 3rd
3rd	3rd, 4th
4th	4th, 5th
5th	2nd, 6th
6th	6th

After removing the "1sts," I found that the 6th button only matched up in the 6th spot in the order. Once again, I went through the list and eliminated the "6ths" from the order column:

Vault Combination, Step Three

Button	Pillar (Order)
1st	1st (confirmed)
2nd	2nd, 3rd
3rd	3rd, 4th
4th	4th, 5th
5th	2nd
6th	6th (confirmed)

This resulted in the 5th button being made second in the order. At this point, the puzzle started to answer itself, like a stubborn knot that's finally been worked loose, or a game of Solitaire in which all of the cards have been turned face-up. If the 5th button was second, then the 2nd button was third. That made the 3rd button fourth, which made the 4th button fifth.

So, I had determined that the solution to the combination was to press the buttons in this order: 1-5-2-3-4-6.

To my great relief, it worked. The massive vault door opened with a throbbing hum of ancient machinery creaking to life. I breathed a sigh of relief. If that solution hadn't worked, I think I would have resorted to banging my head against the door for a while and seeing if that accomplished anything.

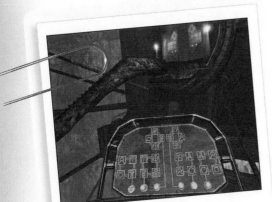

Vault combination—press the buttons in this order: 1st, 5th, 2nd, 3rd, 4th, 6th.

Seventh Journey Cloth

Whoever owned this vault put it to good use—filled with gold, tapestries, etc.

A finely dressed skeleton near a Linking Book; the vault's owner?

Seventh Journey Cloth hung on the wall. Had to do some jumping to reach it.

Mentally exhausted but in high spirits, I ascended the stone stairs and entered the vault, where I saw incalculable riches in piles: gold, tapestries, ornately decorated urns and shields, and much, much more. I'd never heard of any D'ni hoarding wealth like this. From the books I'd read, they seemed to prize scholarship and personal accomplishment above all else.

Of course, all the information I had about the D'ni came either directly or indirectly from the journals of Atrus's wife, Catherine. The three books of D'ni history that the DRC sent me, as well as the <u>Myst</u> games, were based on her accounts of D'ni history, some of which she'd heard third- or fourth-hand. And although I had no reason to believe that Catherine was an unreliable narrator, I also remembered that she had never seen D'ni before its fall, and therefore couldn't be expected to have as complete a view of the society as one might hope. Perhaps Yeesha was right. Perhaps D'ni wasn't as ideal as I'd been led to believe.

In the center of the vault's floor was a Linking Book and a skeleton draped in a fine robe. There was no sign of foul play; the robe was intact, with no bloodstains. The skeleton was also completely intact. There were no indications that this person had been attacked—and who could have reached him inside this vault, anyway?

Linking Book linked to Gallery—why didn't he use it?

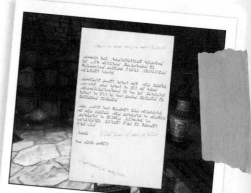

Wished I could read D'ni. Maybe joining the DRC wasn't such a bad idea.

I looked at the Linking Panel of the Book and saw the Gallery. At any point, this person could have linked to the Gallery, which I assumed was in D'ni, and found assistance. Or, he could have linked from the Gallery to the gazebo near the first Kadish Tolesa Journey Cloth. Why didn't he?

There was a note written in D'ni on the floor next to the skeleton. I couldn't read it, but apparently someone had reached this vault before me, because there were comments written in English in the margins. I recognized Yeesha's handwriting on Atrus' note in the Cleft and also in Yeesha's journal in Relto: "Could he realize such failure? What kind of end is this? Impossible unless...." I wished I could have understood what exactly happened here, but I guess I would have to find a DRC translator to do that.

I caught sight of the last Journey Cloth on the rear wall of the vault and jumped up along the crates of valuables until I could reach it. I wanted to make sure that, whatever happened next, I'd be able to return to this vault.

Bahro Cave Door

Bahro Cave door was at the end of a long trip across a guy wire.

As before, Bahro Cave door opened after I got all seven Journey Cloths.

With all seven Journey Cloths found, it was time to locate the Bahro Cave door. I exited the vault, passing a blue switch that could be used to open and close the door.

From the entrance to the vault, I looked back down at the control panel that I used to unlock it, and I saw the Bahro Cave door on a tiny ledge in the vast cavern wall. How was I supposed to reach that?

Returning to the control panel to get a better view of the door, I noticed that one of the thick guy wires that anchored the pathway to the wall stretched down to the ledge near the Bahro Cave door. It was <u>technically</u> wide enough to walk on, but. . . .

I decided to chance it. Although I've never been a fan of great heights, I felt reassured by the Linking Book at my side. If worse came to worst and I fell off of the guy wire, I could "panic link" back to Relto instantly.

Fortunately, my footing was sound, and because I couldn't really see the ground, it didn't bother me all that much. Considering that I'd jumped into a starry void twice already (and was about to do it again, if the pattern held), my tightrope act wasn't as scary as it could have been before I started this journey. At the end of the guy wire, I dropped to the ledge, placed my hand on the Bahro Cave door to open it, and walked inside.

I listened to the familiar squawking and chittering and flapping of giant wings as I inched forward through the darkness. I'd previously assumed that they were the sounds of some sort of giant batlike creature, but it suddenly struck me that these noises could have been the sounds of the Bahro themselves.

After all, I'd heard the same sounds in three different caverns on three different Ages with completely different ecologies. It seemed unlikely that any cave-dwelling creature would be common to Teledahn, Gahreesen, and Kadish Tolesa unless it were capable of linking. And didn't Yeesha imply that the Bahro were "beasts that could link?"

I pressed on through the cave's absolute blackness until I felt the link at the end of it pull me away from Kadish Tolesa.

Back in the Bahro Cave, or something very similar to the last one(s) I'd been in.

Bahro Cave

Once again, I linked to a dimly lit cavern and appeared on the largest of four stone platforms, two of which were missing their Bahro Pillars. I saw another symbol etched into the rock at my feet, next to the Bahro Pillar, as well as the "hand" and "Yeesha" icons on the cavern wall. It was very similar to the other two Bahro Caves I'd linked to, but it couldn't possibly have been the same one . . . could it? Yeesha's voice echoed off of the dimly lit cavern walls:

"You return again. Return to hear more. Return for a third Pillar. It's an interesting cycle, this coming and going—giving and taking. Returning is what you must do.

"For you have torn in half the very being of one of the Least. You have heard their pain—don't falter.

"The bones of Guild Master Kadish speak louder than words. His bones are the bones of D'ni. He clung to the teachings of good King Naghen who required good citizens to cling to their treasure.

"This Kadish you have seen would not give back, would not return, would not let go. He had long been one of the wealthiest of the D'ni, owning more than he could possibly make use of. He built Ages to protect the extra. And when the Fall came, he clung to his possessions over all else. And so you see only death in his vault—extravagant death. It is an image of D'ni.

"The people of D'ni didn't return easily. They only would take, until all was taken from them in the Great Returning, the Fall that destroyed them. D'ni fell only a few hundred years ago. All of it was removed.

"And my journey was similar.

"I could write things that no D'ni had ever dreamed of. My writing smashed barriers held as absolutes for millennia. I could change things, I could move things, I could control things.

I learned beyond my parents, I learned beyond all. I wrote ages against D'ni challengers, Masters of the Art, and they were beaten. I took all that I could hold.

"Only death can conquer pride so strong. For the D'ni and for Yeesha, it was death that moved me to return.

"All died.

"All but the Least, the un-proud. The Bahro considered themselves as dead already. And so they continued to watch D'ni, always ready to give more away.

"And now they will return."

Questions and Answers

Touched hand icon to take the Bahro Pillar.

Dropped into starry abyss to link back to Relto.

Back on Relto, three Bahro Pillars later.

Once again, Yeesha's words raised about as many questions as they answered, but at least I now knew the story behind Kadish Tolesa's vault, or Yeesha's version of it, anyway. The Age was named for its owner, Kadish, whose skeleton I found in the vault. He'd apparently sought sanctuary among his riches when the Fall came to D'ni, but even his tremendous wealth couldn't save him from death's clutches.

On the surface, Kadish seemed to be another damning example of the pride that Yeesha ascribed to D'ni, but I began to wonder if perhaps she wasn't overreaching a bit in this case. The Teledahn slave caverns were a clear-cut case of systematic abuse against a culture, and the Gahreesen Prisons certainly weren't the coziest places I'd ever visited, but Kadish was only one D'ni among hundreds of thousands. From reading The Book of Ti'ana, I knew that D'ni had a fairly rigid class hierarchy, and I knew that some D'ni were rich and some were poor, but from the little I knew of D'ni history, everyone's needs were met. I wasn't sure how Kadish's gluttony, as unappealing a personal quality as it might have been, could be used as an indictment against all of D'ni.

Then again, I'd come to realize that there was a great deal that I didn't know about D'ni, so perhaps Yeesha was right. Perhaps Kadish's behavior was the rule, rather than the exception. Perhaps the proud and wealthy citizens of D'ni did take from the Least until there was nothing left to take. Yeesha certainly seemed to hold a bias against D'ni, but maybe she had good reason for it.

I went back and forth on the matter for some time until, finally, I had to admit that I just didn't have enough information to make a truly informed decision. Maybe Kadish was a glutton who spent his final hours in the false comfort of his riches, or maybe he was just a wealthy D'ni who linked to the safest, most airtight location he knew of in an attempt to avoid the plague. Or maybe he was both. Not for the first time, I found myself wishing that I was affiliated with the DRC and had access to their wealth of historical data. I had no reason to believe that Yeesha was lying to me, but without another perspective on the events, I couldn't say that her version of them was completely accurate either.

Yeesha also revealed a bit more of her own history, but like everything else she'd said, she left a great deal to the imagination. At one point, she apparently returned to D'ni—either the old cavern city or the new D'ni established by Atrus and Catherine after the events of The Book of D'ni—and became one of the most powerful Writers of all time.

At that point, she became "proud," and her pride was "conquered" by death. Whose death? She didn't say, only that "all died." Did she make some mistake in her Writing that doomed everyone around her? I considered the possibility that the "pride" she ascribed to herself, that she so loathed, was a psychological reaction to the death that had obviously profoundly affected her, a sort of survivor's guilt.

Was it then that she met the Bahro? How did she meet them? And what frame of mind was she in when she did?

As I transcribed Yeesha's speech, something else stood out. She said that I had "torn in half the very being of one of the Least," that I had "heard their pain," but that I should continue on the journey.

I had "torn" one of the Bahro in half? While looking at the two remaining Bahro Pillars, Yeesha's words started to make more sense. If I understood her correctly, while moving the Bahro Pillars from the cave (or caves) to Relto, I was actually moving the essence of a single Bahro. If that were true, then the Bahro that I was moving was now caught between two Ages, which certainly didn't sound like a pleasant situation. The screeching and squawking I'd heard when I entered the Bahro Caves—was that the sound of a Bahro in pain?

I was more determined than ever to finish Yeesha's journey, if not to finally understand what it was all about, then at least to end the suffering of the Bahro I was moving. I touched the hand icon to transport the Bahro Pillar to Relto, and then I walked off of the stone ledge and dropped into the starry void below.

Eder Gira and Eder Kemo

Eder Gira

Eder Gira and Eder Kemo were two closely related Ages that made up the fourth and final part of my journey. Unlike the other Ages I had explored, Eder Kemo and Eder Gira had seven Journey Cloths between them, not seven Journey Cloths in a single Age. The two Eders (must remember to look up what that word means) would also prove to contain some of the most physically demanding parts of my journey.

Upper Gira

Eder Gira's pedestal was the near left one from the hut entrance.

Whew! Should have worn shorts!

With the Bahro Pillars from Teledahn, Gahreesen, and Kadish Tolesa recovered, only the Pillar from Eder Gira and Eder Kemo was left. Only one pedestal remained in Relto without a Bahro Pillar on top of it, the near left pedestal (as I stood with my back to the hut). I opened the pedestal, retrieved the Linking Book, and linked into Eder Gira.

As soon as I arrived in the Age, I was assaulted with a wave of blistering heat; I had appeared in the middle of a hardened lava flow, near two hissing fumaroles that discharged puffs of steam at regular intervals.

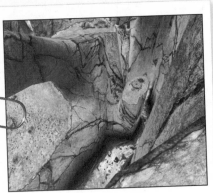

Looking down at molten river from hardened lava path.

One of six fumaroles. Stepping on the foot pedal opened or closed the cap.

I walked onto the hardened lava path, which stretched high above a deep canyon. An angry red ribbon of lava lined the bottom of the canyon. For a moment, I feared that the Age was unstable and in its death throes, but the sight of waterfalls in the distance reassured me. I was no geologist, but it seemed to be that a world on the verge of self-destruction wouldn't have such beautiful cascades of water or such a clear blue sky.

I walked along the entire expanse of what I would later come to know as Upper Gira and discovered that it was essentially two large rocky plateaus with a land bridge spanning the river of lava below.

Six steaming fumaroles were scattered across Upper Gira: two on each plateau, one at one end of the land bridge, and another sitting on a pinnacle above the lava river. All six fumaroles had caps that were triggered by foot switches; one press of the switch covered the fumarole, and a second press opened it again. When I linked into Eder Gira, all six were open. I noticed that when I closed a fumarole, the pressure of the open fumaroles' steamy discharge increased. When all six covers were closed, however, the pressure was too great, and the fumaroles all blew their covers back into the open position.

FIRST JOURNEY CLOTH

Saw the first Journey Cloth from a distance, hanging above a small ledge over the lava river.

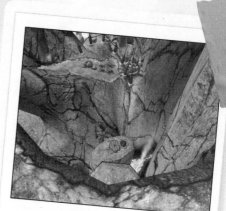

Walked to edge of plateau and dropped off of it onto Journey Cloth ledge.

During my exploration of Upper Gira, I crossed the land bridge to the plateau opposite the one I'd linked onto. While standing at the end of the land bridge that was nearer the still-distant waterfalls, I turned and looked back at the plateau onto which I'd linked. Jutting out from the plateau's vertical rock wall, just beyond the pinnacle with the fumarole on it, was a tiny ledge. Above the ledge hung the first Journey Cloth I'd seen in the Age.

I headed back across the land bridge to the plateau onto which I'd linked, then climbed to the highest point of the plateau that overlooked the lava river. The ledge with the Journey Cloth was directly below me.

I walked carefully off of the plateau and safely fell onto the ledge. The heat was much more intense down here. I didn't plan on sticking around.

SECOND JOURNEY CLOTH

Jumped to the pinnacle and shut the fumarole.

From the pinnacle, I made a running jump to the edge of the plateau.

Closed both fumaroles near where I landed from the pinnacle jump.

There was nowhere to go from the ledge except onto the nearby pinnacle with the fumarole. I examined the pinnacle carefully and mentally calculated the difference between the ledge I was on and the top of the pinnacle below me. I concluded that a jump would overshoot the pinnacle and land me in the lava below (of course, I would "panic link" back to Relto before I hit it).

Instead, I ran off of the ledge toward the pinnacle and landed right in the middle of it. Between the molten river below me and the fumarole right in front of me, it was ridiculously hot. I immediately stepped on the fumarole's foot switch to try to cool things down a bit.

Looking around, I decided that there was only one ledge that I had any chance of leaping to: the edge of the plateau opposite the one I'd linked onto. With my Linking Book at the ready for a panic link, I ran toward the plateau, jumped, and just barely made it to the other side.

I took a moment to wipe the sweat from my brow and relax in the relative cool of the plateau. I didn't know quite what else to do, so I decided to play with the fumaroles for a little while. There were two more fumaroles on the plateau I had just jumped to, right next to each other in front of a small rock wall. On a whim, I closed them both.

Crossed the land bridge and shut the fumarole at the other end of it.

Saw second Journey Cloth on a ledge high above my link-in point, above a fumarole.

I then crossed the land bridge and returned to the plateau I'd linked onto, closing the fumarole at the end of the land bridge as I passed it. With four fumaroles closed, I could hear the pressure mounting. The lid on the fumarole I'd just shut was shaking, but it held fast.

I continued walking along the path toward my link-in point, and that's when I saw the second Journey Cloth, high above the exact location that I appeared in when I linked into Eder Gira. It hung on the side of a steep pillar, just above a tiny ledge. I couldn't reach the ledge from the pathway, but I noticed that there was a fumarole at the base of the pillar. I had another crazy idea.

Shut the fumarole near the one directly underneath the Journey Cloth.

With 5 of 6 fumaroles closed, the last one shot me up to the ledge w/ the Journey Cloth.

Four of the six fumaroles were already shut. I closed the one not directly below the Journey Cloth. Now the fumarole under the second Journey Cloth was the only open one.

Cautiously, I extended my hand over the blast of steam. I was pleasantly surprised to find it warm but not scalding, which gave me the confidence to try my next experiment: I stepped into the steam vent of the only open fumarole. With the next blast of steam, I shot straight up into the air and landed on the ledge with the second Journey Cloth.

Lower Gira

After touching the second Journey Cloth, I dropped down to the plateau below me

Opened the fumarole in front of the short rock wall on the other side of Upper Gira.

Returned to fumarole under 2nd
Journey Cloth and shut it.

Used fumarole in front of
small rock wall to launch me
over the wall.

and crossed the land bridge back to the other plateau. Having just launched myself onto the Journey Cloth ledge, I was curious to see if I could use the fumaroles to launch myself over the small rock wall near the pair of fumaroles on this plateau as well.

I opened the fumarole directly in front of the rock wall, and then I returned to the first plateau and closed the fumarole that had launched me up to the second Journey Cloth. (Had I done these two steps in the opposite order, all six fumaroles would have popped their tops, and I would have had to start all over again.)

Now, with the fumarole in front of the small rock wall being the only open fumarole in Upper Gira, I returned to it and stood on it. Once again, the steam blast shot me up into the air, and I cleared the rock wall with ease.

Shrine containing Linking Book to Eder Kemo.

Water, sweet water!

Linking Stone near Linking Book.

A pathway on the other side of the rock wall led into the section of Eder Gira that I dubbed Lower Gira. Compared to the relentless heat of Upper Gira, Lower Gira was a paradise. Although the ground still radiated the warmth of the nearby lava flow, the waterfalls feeding Lower Gira's crystal-clear lake gave me the perfect chance to cool off and refresh myself. The raylike fish that swam around me didn't seem to mind my company.

The bones of a mammoth beast were planted along the walkways of Lower Gira, like some sort of macabre decoration. Straight ahead along the baked dirt pathway was a small shrine with an open Linking Book on it.

Just past the Linking Book shrine was a small brook that flowed away from the larger pond and off the edge of Lower Gira as a waterfall. On the other side of this brook was a gray boulder with a Linking Stone lying up against it. Because I hadn't found a Journey Cloth in Lower Gira yet, I decided against using it to link just yet.

Caverns behind waterfalls.

The torches inside of them still worked.

Two waterfalls crashed into the pond next to the Linking Stone, and I saw open caverns beyond them. Walking around the side of the waterfall closest to the Linking Stone, I was able to jump into the cavern from the pathway.

Inside the cavern, I found two ancient torches that—miraculously—still worked. I turned the knobs on the top of them, and they lit the inside of the cavern with a bright yellow glow.

The only other item of interest in the cavern was a hexagonal wooden basket, which I found between the two cavern openings behind the waterfalls. I nudged it into the water to see if it would float. It didn't; it sank like a stone. (I didn't realize it until later, but that basket was going to be a tremendous help to me during my journey.)

Kicked a basket from the cavern into the water. Sunk like a stone.

Unlit tunnel leading from the cavern was too dark to enter.

There was also an unlit tunnel leading up from one side of the cavern, but it was so dark in there that I found myself stumbling around and almost falling back down the way I came in. I resolved to go back in later, but only once I'd found some source of light.

Eder Kemo

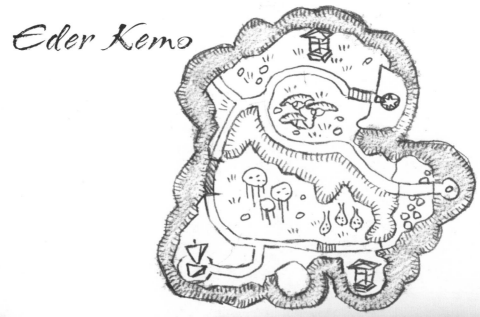

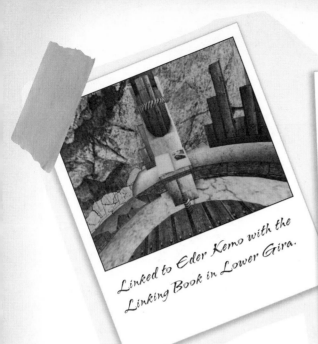

Linked to Eder Kemo with the Linking Book in Lower Gira.

Eder Kemo was a Garden Age with a completely different climate.

I had seen all there was to see of Lower Gira for the moment. I now had two options for continuing my journey: the Linking Stone near the waterfall or the Linking Book in the shrine. Because every Linking Stone that I'd used so far required me to link back to Relto after using it, I decided to use the Linking Book, because I hadn't yet found a Journey Cloth that would bring me back to Lower Gira. I placed my hand on the Linking Panel and found myself transported to Eder Kemo.

Eder Kemo was the exact opposite of Eder Gira. Instead of Eder Gira's cracked volcanic pathways and oppressive heat, Eder Kemo offered a lush garden paradise. Where Eder Gira's sky was cloudless and offered no relief from the sun's heat, Eder Kira's appeared to be on the verge of a rainstorm.

URU
AGES BEYOND MYST.
Prima's Official Travel Guide

Third Journey Cloth

I walked along the pathway from the link-in point and followed it into the verdant courtyard. Veering off of the pathway, I walked around the back of the enormous stone pillar in the nearby rock garden and found the third Journey Cloth for my Eder Gira/Eder Kemo journey.

Found the third Journey Cloth on the opposite side of the large stone pillar in the courtyard.

Fourth Journey Cloth

Stood in "bamboo" grove's gazebo until the rain stopped.

Found 4th Journey Cloth in a corner of the "bamboo" grove.

After activating the third Journey Cloth, I turned around to face the small grove of bamboo-like trees behind me. An elegant four-sided gazebo sat in the center of the grove, which was fortunate for me, because I heard the rumble of thunder in the distance. I stepped under the gazebo's protective canopy just as the first drops of rain began to fall.

The storm was short but intense. As soon as it was over, I took a closer look at the grove of trees, and that's when I saw the fourth Journey Cloth tucked away in a small alcove in the corner of the grove. I activated it without delay.

Eder Kemo Flora and Fauna

Etchings on the wall near Eder Kemo fountain.

Giant slug-tick thing! They're all along the walls here! Gross!

I took a moment to investigate the fountain near the third and fourth Journey Cloths. I didn't find anything that helped me on my journey, but I did notice several crude drawings along the cliff wall. They seemed to represent people engaged in some kind of activity in Eder Kemo's gardens, but I couldn't decipher their meanings.

As I studied the etchings, something moving along the cliff ledge caught the corner of my eye. I looked up and jumped back in disgust—a pair of enormous, bloated, insectlike creatures hung directly above my head! They looked like a cross between a tick and a slug, and they were at least as big as I was. I left the area around the fountain immediately after snapping a picture of them.

I hate bugs. Especially bugs that are bigger than me.

After catching sight of the two near the fountain, I noticed more of them along the upper ledges of Eder Kemo. All of a sudden, it didn't seem like the lush paradise I'd originally thought it to be. I resolved to finish up my exploration as quickly as possible.

Bahro Cave door, in the center of Eder Kemo.

Etching near Bahro Cave door.

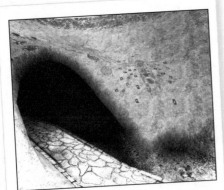

Etchings on tunnel entrance— humanoid figure surrounded by yellow dots?

Heading back down the pathway, away from the fountain, I saw the Bahro Cave door to my right. There were some more indecipherable etchings on the stone wall next to it, and another one of those giant slug-ticks above it.

I continued down the path through a tunnel, the entrance of which was decorated with more etchings. One of the etchings depicted a person surrounded by little yellow dots. I wasn't sure what these meant either, but I figured that they had to serve some purpose.

"Brain trees."

Glowing bugs around brain trees hid when the rain came.

On the other side of the tunnel was another forest of trees, but these were like nothing I'd ever seen before. The tops of them looked like giant pink brains, and several "tassels" hung down from them. Flitting from tree to tree was a cluster of glowing yellow insects; they seemed to be pollinating the tassels. I wondered if the etching of the person surrounded by the yellow dots was supposed to represent these insects, and I wondered if the drawing was supposed to be a warning or not.

As I watched the glowing bugs from a distance, the sky began to darken again. I stood underneath a brain tree for protection from the rain. As the rain began to fall, the glow bugs zipped into the top of a brain tree and remained there until the storm ended.

Fifth Journey Cloth

Hieroglyphics on garden rest area.

Fifth Journey Cloth hung on the side of a lamppost overlooking the rest area.

Across from the largest grove of brain trees, where I'd seen the glow bugs, was a rounded rest area with a naturally rounded stone wall. More hieroglyphics were drawn onto the walls. I photographed them all.

As I walked on top of the stone wall to get a better angle for the photos, I saw the Age's fifth Journey Cloth hanging on the lamppost that hung over the rest area. I activated it; five down, two to go.

Sixth Journey Cloth

Across the garden from the fifth Journey Cloth was an amazing stone sculpture, seemingly made of gray stone and gold.

Rotating levitating sculpture.

The huge scale and elegant geometric design of the sculpture was impressive enough, but the entire sculpture also levitated about five feet off its pedestal and rotated in the air, with no wires or other support. Its existence spoke of the incredible resources at the disposal of whoever created this Age.

Another etching on the wall behind the sculpture.

Behind the sculpture was another hieroglyph of a humanoid figure wearing what seemed to be a tiger-striped vest. At its left hand was some sort of boxy device—one of the torches I'd seen in Eder Gira, perhaps? I stopped pondering the image as soon as I saw another giant tick-slug overhead.

I really, really hate bugs.

Puffers.

6th Journey Cloth, in a corner of the puffer grove.

I headed back down the pathway past the brain trees, where I saw another grove of enormous teardrop-shaped plants that I dubbed "puffers," after the way that they swelled up and puffed out clouds of pollen into the air.

To one side of the puffer grove was another gazebo, and on a rock wall near the gazebo was the sixth Journey Cloth of the Age. I activated it and then continued down the path.

Eder Gira Linking Book

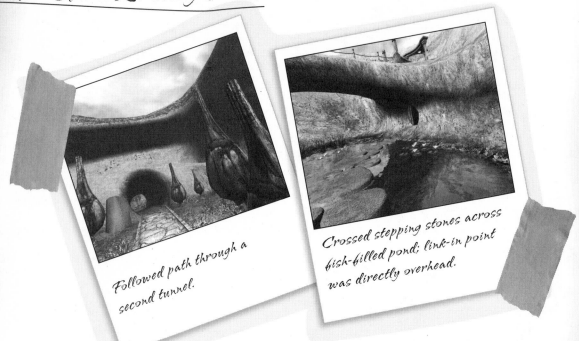

Followed path through a second tunnel.

Crossed stepping stones across fish-filled pond; link-in point was directly overhead.

Alcove w/ Lower Gira Linking Book at the end of the path.

At the end of the path was another tunnel, and beyond that tunnel was a series of stepping stones across a pond. In the pond swam the fish that I assumed were the inspiration for the pattern for Eder Kemo's pedestal in Relto. A land bridge stretched high overhead across the pond, and I recognized it as my link-in point from Eder Gira.

I crossed the pond and entered a small alcove with a Linking Book in it. A quick glance at the Linking Panel showed the waterfalls of Lower Gira. I placed my hand on it and linked back to Eder Gira.

Linking Stone

Used Lower Gira Linking Stone.

Linked to DRC field office on a D'ni city rooftop.

Lots of journals and other info to read.

The Eder Gira Linking Book brought me right back to Lower Gira, near the temple with the Linking Book to Eder Kemo. Now that I had activated Linking Cloths in Eder Kemo, I decided to use the Linking Stone in Lower Gira.

Placing my hand on the Linking Stone, I felt myself vanish from Eder Gira and reappear in a DRC field office on a rooftop in D'ni. Although I couldn't leave the rooftop to explore D'ni itself, I had an excellent view of several of the larger buildings through a nearby telescope.

URU
AGES BEYOND MYST.
Prima's Official Travel Guide

The field office was a virtual treasure trove of information about the D'ni. I found no fewer than 13 DRC notebooks full of information about D'ni customs, social structures, and ancient kings, all of which I copied into my journal.

The journals made for some very interesting reading and filled in a few more of the holes in my understanding of the life and times of D'ni. But two notes left at the site were of more immediate interest to me:

EDITOR'S NOTE:
All of these journals have been reprinted by kind permission of the DRC and appear in "Appendix B: DRC Research" at the end of this guide.

Where the heck is my book? And why did someone take it in the first place!

—Nick

Nick's first note.

Apparently there was another journal to be found. I'd have to keep my eyes open for it.

Nick's second note.

This note was found on top of a scrap of a Journey Cloth. It was interesting to see that the DRC didn't want their explorers to activate any of the Journey Cloths. Were they aware of Yeesha and the Bahro Pillars? Judging from the way Nick talked about the Journey Cloths activating the Bahro Cave doors, it would seem that they would have had to be aware of them.

I was also intrigued by the way that Nick described the reappearance of the Journey Cloth after he removed it, just as Douglas Sharper's Linking Stone kept reappearing in the place that he'd taken it from. I wondered what Nick meant when he said that removing the Journey Cloth from the wall was "scary."

Linking Book to Eder Kemo appeared next to Eder Gira Linking Book in my Relto Library.

After copying over all of the journals (which took several hours and cramped my hand up something fierce), I used my Linking Book to return to Relto. When I got there, I noticed that a fifth Linking Book had appeared in my Library. Eder Gira's was the red book, fourth from the left. But there was also a green Linking Book for Eder Kemo to the right of Eder Gira's.

I wondered how that was possible, but since I had no answers, I pulled out the Eder Kemo Linking Book and used the Journey Cloth bookmark to return to the area near the puffer gazebo.

Glow Bugs

Walked through the cloud of glow bugs in the brain trees.

A dozen or so glow bugs stayed with me, as long as I didn't run, jump, or go in water.

I had officially run out of ideas about where to go next. I'd explored every square inch of Eder Kemo's gardens, and there was nothing left to see in Eder Gira, except that pitch-black tunnel in the cavern behind Lower Gira's waterfall. But without a light source, I couldn't explore it at all.

It was then that I remembered the glowing insects in the brain tree grove. They didn't give off much light, but I didn't need much. And that mural on the tunnel entrance showed a person surrounded by the glow bugs—I wondered if I could get them to follow me?

I stepped into the middle of the brain tree grove and, having no better plan, walked straight into the middle of the cloud of glow bugs. To my surprise, about a dozen of them started flitting around me in a playful orbit. At first, I stood completely still, afraid that they might decide to swarm and sting me, or crawl in my ear and lay eggs, or any of the other nasty things that bugs do to people. But these glow bugs seemed content to just follow me wherever I walked.

Okay. Maybe I don't hate <u>all</u> bugs.

I had the glow bugs, but could I keep them with me? After about half an hour of experimentation with the glow bugs, I catalogued a list of things that would cause them to leave my presence. First, although they would link with me, I would lose some of them if I jumped and all of them if I ran. Also, the bugs were hydrophobic; they couldn't stand water, whether it was Eder Kemo's rain or Eder Gira's pond and waterfalls. Even the steam from Eder Gira's volcanic vents would drive them away.

Returned to Lower Gira and pushed hexagonal basket into narrow creek to cross it w/out jumping.

I returned to Lower Gira and started to plan my strategy for getting the glow bugs into the cavern with me. As things stood, I needed to make two jumps from the link-in point from Eder Kemo if I wanted to reach the cavern without touching the water: one jump across the brook, and another into the cavern. The problem was, I'd lose all of the bugs after the second jump. I needed to eliminate one of those jumps so that I'd have enough bugs to light the tunnel.

URU

AGES BEYOND MYST.

Prima's Official Travel Guide

I remembered the hexagonal basket I'd pushed out of the cavern and into the water earlier. It was just wide enough to serve as a stepping stone across the brook, thus eliminating the brook jump! I returned to Lower Gira and pushed the basket into position so that it served as a makeshift footbridge across the brook.

With that done, I linked back to Eder Kemo and collected a swarm of glow bugs. Timing my movements carefully, I made sure that I was never standing out in the open when the rain came, and I never moved at any speed faster than a walk. I returned to the Linking Book at the end of the pathway and linked back to Lower Gira.

Returned to Eder Kemo, got a swarm of bugs, linked back to Lower Gira, and walked across basket in brook.

Jumped across water into cavern behind waterfall. Lost half my glow bugs, but still had 5 or 6.

I walked around the steam vent in front of my link-in point and then walked over the basket, which did its job perfectly. I reached the other side of the brook with all of my glow bugs still swarming around me.

I stood as close to the cavern entrance as I could without setting foot in the water, and then I jumped into it without running toward it. Half of my glow bugs departed, but I still had five or six around me.

Walked through tunnel; glow bugs gave off just enough light to see.

Lit the torch at the end of that section of tunnel.

I walked into the tunnel and saw that the glow bugs' light was just bright enough for me to make my way through the darkness. When the tunnel ended in a small junction, I lit the torch that I found in the middle of the cave.

Pulled lever to open wooden door in the junction; walked through tunnel on the other side.

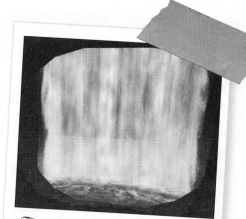

Tunnel ended in waterfall. Doubled back to the last torch.

There was another tunnel stretching up into the darkness, as well as a closed wooden door that blocked off another tunnel. I pulled the lever near the door to open it and then proceeded through to the other side.

The tunnel beyond the door ended in a cavern with an exit to the waterfall outside. Not wanting to lose my glow bugs, I doubled back to the room with the lantern in it and went into the tunnel that I hadn't explored yet.

This tunnel led out to a narrow stone ledge that ran along the outside of the caverns. It was interrupted by a gap caused by a small waterfall. Although I could jump over it, I'd lose the rest of my glow bugs.

I decided to return to the cavern beyond the door, the one that ended in a waterfall. Although it meant losing my glow bugs, I decided it was worth exploring, and so I exited the cavern.

I was now standing at the top of the twin waterfalls I'd seen from the ground. Standing at the edge of the waterfalls, I could look out and see the main part of Lower Gira. I walked around to the other waterfall and entered the cavern beyond it.

Other tunnel leading from last torch led to an exterior pathway with a gap in it.

Backtracked to pathway beyond the wooden door, followed it out to the top of the twin waterfalls.

Pushed two hexagonal baskets from the nearby cavern over the waterfall.

Positioned hexagonal baskets between shore and lower cavern entrance.

Inside this waterfall were two more of those hexagonal baskets I'd used as a stepping stone over the brook. I realized that if I pushed these baskets over the waterfall, I could use them as stepping stones to enter the lower cavern without needing to jump. That way, I could enter the caverns with all of my glow bugs, jump over the gap in the stone ledge I'd seen earlier, and still have a few bugs left to explore anything that might be on the other side of the ledge.

With a bit of effort, I kicked the baskets over the waterfall, and then I dropped into the water after them. It was much quicker than taking the cavern path back down! Moving the baskets into position also required some finesse, but once they were there, I realized that my plan was sound, and that I'd be able to enter the cavern with a full complement of glow bugs.

Nick's Book and Yeesha Page

I linked back to Eder Kemo, got another swarm of glow bugs, and walked toward the

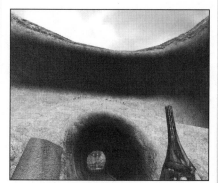

Found Nick's missing journal above Eder Kemo tunnel that led to Lower Gira Linking Book.

From the journal location, I turned around and saw a Yeesha Page on a nearby ledge.

Leapt from tunnel mouth to boulder to ledge to reach Yeesha Page.

Eder Gira Linking Book. However, as I did, I noticed something sitting above the entrance to the tunnel near the puffers; it looked like a blue notebook.

I took a quick detour and scrambled up onto the tunnel entrance. There I found Nick's missing notebook, surrounded by some etchings I didn't understand. I picked up the notebook and read it. It contained some sort of historical fable about a D'ni king named Shomat who lured his treacherous brothers to death in a garden filled with savage beasts. I wondered if Eder Kemo was meant to be that garden?

EDITOR'S NOTE:
This journal was returned to the DRC and is reprinted in its entirety by their kind permission in "Appendix B: DRC Research."

After finishing the notebook, I turned around and saw something on a ledge that overlooked the puffers—it looked like a sheet of paper.

From the ledge I was on, I hopped onto a rock near the ledge with the sheet of paper, and from there I leapt again to reach the paper. It was another Yeesha Page, one that added a rug to my hut in Relto, as well as some ornamentation to the exterior of the hut itself. I tucked it away in my Linking Book, went back for more glow bugs, and headed toward the Eder Gira Linking Book.

Seventh Journey Cloth

Returned to Eder Kemo for more glow bugs, linked back to Lower Gira, and walked across baskets to lower cavern w/out jumping.

Walked along tunnels until I reached the gap in the outdoor ledge; leapt over the gap & still kept 5 or 6 bugs w/ me.

Path ended in a dark tunnel with a torch in it: lit the torch.

After finishing the journal, I linked back to Lower Gira with my glow bugs in tow. Thanks to the three baskets I'd placed, I was able to enter the cavern behind the waterfall without losing a single glow bug.

From the cavern, I returned to the stone ledge and leapt across the waterfall gap (without running), landing on the other side of the ledge with half of my glow bugs still surrounding me.

I followed the ledge as it curved to the right and led straight into a tunnel. I knew those glow bugs would come in handy! Inside the tunnel was another torch. I turned it on, and a yellow glow illuminated the round stone walls.

Last Journey Cloth hung on the wall of the tunnel.

The seventh and final Journey Cloth hung on the wall of the cavern. I activated it and retraced my steps to the Eder Kemo Linking Book in Lower Gira. After linking back to Eder Kemo, I followed the path to the Bahro Cave door and opened it. I heard the sounds of the Bahro inside, and I decided to go back for some glow bugs, just to see if I could get a glimpse of the Bahro. But when I stepped into the cavern, even the glow bugs' light was swallowed whole by the Bahro Cave's dark embrace, and they fled from me. I continued walking into the darkness.

Bahro Cave

When I appeared in the Bahro Cave, I found it exactly the same—with the same contradictions—as my previous three visits. Once again, I stood on the largest of four ledges, and mine was the only ledge with a Bahro Pillar and a symbol etched into its floor. I turned on my tape recorder as Yeesha began to speak:

Returned to the Bahro Cave door in Eder Kemo.

"Many stories were there for the D'ni to learn from, but they didn't hear them. The ancient tales of Thu'it's Ocean. Or, of course, the story of King Shomat and his brothers, which even speaks of gardens and death, but no one truly listened. The Garden Ages of the proud are beautiful, but they are built on the backs of the Least.

"The Ages like Kemo and Gira are a sampling of the playthings of D'ni. With disregard, the Least were stripped from their homes. The lives in those Ages were consumed, and the D'ni gave nothing back. And whatever is not given back will be taken.

"The journeys are complete. Now take the final Pillar. Take it, but hear all I've said. It's the whispers and murmurs that reveal the simple truths. You hold the precious soul of a Bahro in your Age—in your hand. Such things are not meant to be held.

"Do what I do.

"I have learned things, seen things, written things they never thought possible. I have seen the real treasures that are protected by the petty fences of their rules, I have found the precious gold buried deep beneath the weighty mountains of their laws.

"This is my journey too. I am returning what has been given. These years I've spent, this path I've traveled, this gift I've been given, this purpose weighs on me—my burden—the legacy of my father Atrus. For we are shaping D'ni; we will mold what comes after. We cannot keep the power and the pride from ruining this new D'ni, but we can prepare those who will read between the lines.

"The Least are returning. The stream in the Cleft is returning. Life is returning. The fissure is returning.

"The circle will be completed when you give back what you have taken. You must return."

Questions and Answers

Touched hand icon to take final Bahro Pillar.

Dropped into starry abyss to return to Relto.

I reflected on Yeesha's words in the flickering blue light of the dim cavern and was disappointed to hear that, as close as I was to the end of my journey, she wouldn't stop speaking in riddles. I still had as many questions as ever, though some were new questions, replacing ones that she had indirectly answered.

Yeesha strongly implied that there were living, sentient creatures inhabiting Eder Gira and/or Eder Kemo before the D'ni moved in. That didn't seem to be too much of a stretch of the imagination, because the pictograms on the rock walls of Eder Kemo were definitely made by a people much less advanced than the D'ni.

The Least who lived in Eder Kemo before the D'ni arrived were "stripped from their homes," much like the corrupt King Shomat commissioned his treacherous brothers to exterminate the beast-men (<u>bahro</u>, in the generic sense) from his Garden Age in the story I read in Nick's notebook.

But to play devil's advocate, I did notice in the Shomat story that two D'ni objected to Shomat's ruthlessness. Shomat's advisor, Lemash, recommended that the Linking Book to the Garden Age be burned, as was the D'ni custom if an Age was found to be inhabited. Lemash reminded his king that under D'ni law, inhabited Ages were not for D'ni use. Shomat's rejection of Lemash's plea actually reinforced the virtue of D'ni culture, in my mind.

Also, after Shomat had disposed of his brothers, he ordered the Grand Master Kenri to change the Garden Age Linking Book so that all of its inhabitants would die. Although Kenri bowed to the will of his king, the story states that Kenri knew that what he did was wrong, "and his life was filled with turmoil until he died." Again, this seemed to reinforce the idea that individual D'ni could occasionally be corrupt and abuse their power, but the fundamental code of D'ni conduct was sound.

Of course, if the Bahro were the original inhabitants of Eder Kemo, and if their land was stolen from them, it seemed only right to try to make some sort of amends. Because the D'ni were all but extinct, whatever reparations were made to the Bahro would not be made at the expense of the D'ni. I saw no reason not to continue assisting Yeesha in "returning" the Bahro, whatever that meant.

With the fourth Bahro Pillar in my possession, I would have a single Bahro soul in my custody, according to Yeesha. But what was I supposed to do with it? She said that I had to give back what I had taken, that I must return. But "return" in what sense? Return the Bahro Pillars, or return to the Bahro Caves from which I took them?

I started to wonder if that wasn't an either/or question at all. Was Yeesha actually telling me to do both, to return to the Bahro Cave in each Age _and_ to touch the hand icon on the wall to return the Bahro Pillar to it? It seemed as if I would be undoing a lot of work if I did so, but it was also the only idea I had at the moment.

If I was correct, I would apparently be the cause of several "returns": the return of the Bahro, of the Cleft stream, of life, and of "the fissure." I wasn't sure what all of that meant, exactly, but I resolved that I would soon find out. I touched the hand icon to move the Bahro Pillar to Relto, and then I dropped into the starry expanse below the ledge to return to Relto myself.

The Returnings

Returning the Bahro Pillars

Return to Teledahn

All four pedestals rose into the air when I returned to Relto from Eder Kemo.

Linked back to Teledahn and entered Bahro Cave door.

As soon as I linked back to Relto after retrieving the fourth Bahro Pillar from the Bahro Cave at Eder Kemo, I saw all four Relto pedestals rise up from the ground. It was time to test my hypothesis, to see if returning the Bahro Pillars was what I was supposed to do to complete the journey.

I went into the hut and selected the Teledahn Linking Book, second from the left in my Library. Because the last Journey Cloth I'd touched in that Age was the one right outside the Bahro Cave door, I used the Journey Cloth bookmark as a shortcut to return there.

Bahro Cave now had an orange glow, rather than blue.

Touching the hand icon returned the Bahro Pillar to the Bahro Cave.

The Bahro Cave door opened at my touch, and I walked to the end of it to appear in the Bahro Cave. But it was a different cave. The light from the censers overhead was orange, not blue, and the stone ledge I stood on was larger than the ledges I'd stood on previously.

Some things had remained the same. The Yeesha icon on the wall replayed the message I'd heard from her during my first visit to the Teledahn Bahro Cave. Touching the hand icon returned the Bahro Pillar to the rock ledge.

As I touched the hand icon to return the pillar, a sound that I can only describe as a shimmering roar reverberated throughout the cavern. I took that as a signal that I had accomplished something. Whether it was a good something or a bad something, I'd find out soon enough.

Dropped off of ledge to return to Relto; bottom of cave was different.

After returning the Bahro Pillar, I prepared to fall into the starry expanse below the ledge, just as I'd done four times previously. But when I looked down below the ledge, instead of stars, I saw an orange fog lining the bottom of the cave. This was definitely not the Bahro Cave I'd been in previously.

I thought back to the giant stone slab that I had seen in the D'ni balcony, which I had reached by using a Linking Stone in Gahreesen. I pulled out a picture of it to remind myself of the hieroglyphics etched into it. Now it was starting to make sense. The slab had indicated two Bahro Caves, one with stars under it and one with clouds under it. Somehow, by retrieving all four of the Bahro Pillars by completing the journey through the four Ages, I had changed the location that the Bahro Caves linked to.

Things were starting to come together, but I still had three more Bahro Pillars to return. My Linking Book still didn't work in the cave, so I crossed my fingers and hoped that the method of escape was the same as I walked off of the ledge and fell into the swirling orange mists below.

Return to Gahreesen

Outline of a crack in the earth appeared between Relto pedestals.

Linked to Gahreesen and entered Bahro Cave door.

I disappeared from the cave and reappeared in Relto. As I did, I saw the jagged outline of a crack in the earth flash for an instant between the four pedestals. I recognized the shape of it—it was the same shape as the star fissure that Atrus's Myst Linking Book had fallen through at the start of the events in <u>Myst</u>, which was the same fissure seen in <u>Riven</u>. It couldn't be a simple coincidence. When Yeesha talked about the "fissure" returning, this is what she meant.

I hurried back into my hut and linked to Gahreesen via the Journey Cloth shortcut that put me atop the pinnacle between the two rotating buildings. A couple of careful jumps took me down to the Bahro Cave door, which I opened and entered.

Reappeared in Bahro Cave; seemed to be repairing ledges as I moved Bahro Pillars to them.

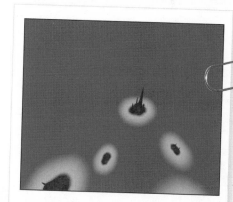

What were those "islands" in the orange mist below the cave?

Once again, I appeared in the orange glow of the new Bahro Cave. Unlike my experience with the original blue Bahro Caves, however, I was certain that I had linked into the same cave that I'd visited from Teledahn. Directly across from me was the ledge on which I'd replaced the Teledahn Bahro Pillar, but the ledge was still the same size and shape as it was when I first visited it. When I visited the blue Bahro Caves, the ledge on which I stood was always the largest, but now I stood on a ledge that was the same size as the first one I'd stepped onto. It seemed

Prima's Official Travel Guide

that, as I replaced the Bahro Pillars in this cave, I was also restoring the ledges to their original sizes and shapes.

I replaced the second Bahro Pillar, which triggered the same sound I'd heard before. Having done so, I dropped into the swirling mist to return to Relto. As I fell, I saw what seemed to be small rocky islands sticking up from the mist. Or perhaps they were the tips of mountains?

Upon reappearing in Relto, I saw the outline of the fissure grow more distinct. I went into my hut, selected the third book from the left, and linked via the Journey Cloth bookmark to Kadish Tolesa.

Return to Kadish Tolesa

Returned to Kadish Tolesa; entered Bahro Cave door.

After returning the Pillar and linking back to Relto, the crack between the pedestals grew more distinct.

Although I didn't relish making the guy wire tightrope walk from the vault control panel to the Bahro Cave door again, it was the only way to reach the cave and return the third Bahro Pillar. Also, being so near the end of my journey (and so curious to see the Relto (fissure) gave me the boost of intestinal fortitude I needed to cross the guy wire quickly and safely.

After entering the Bahro Cave door and linking to the cave itself, I saw that my earlier hypothesis about restoring the rock ledges was correct. The ledge onto which I linked had widened dramatically, and its edges rested right up against the other two ledges I'd visited. I could now walk three-quarters of the way around the Bahro Cave.

I replaced the third Bahro Pillar and dropped into the mists below. Just before reaching the point where I linked back to Relto, I looked at the islands in the dim orange glow below me and had a flash of insight; could they be the islands of the city of D'ni? The orange glow certainly reminded me of the orange glow of the underground lake's algae. But if that was D'ni below, where was this cave?

Return to Eder Kemo

Linked to Eder Kemo, entered Bahro Cave door, returned Bahro Pillar.

Made a note of the symbols on the floor of the Bahro Cave.

Once again, as I returned to Relto, the outline of the fissure grew thicker and bolder. It now looked as if I could open it by standing on it and jumping repeatedly, which I tried, but to no avail. I was convinced that the restoration of the final Bahro Pillar would open it, however, so I chose the fifth book in my Library and linked to Eder Kemo.

Eder Kemo's Bahro Cave door led me back to the Bahro Cave for a final time. All four ledges had been restored, and I could walk all the way around the cave freely, save for the small gap in the center of the room that I must fall through to leave the cave.

After restoring the final Bahro Pillar, I copied down the symbols etched into the floor. They looked like the symbols I'd entered into the Cleft Imager at the beginning of my journey. If there was one thing I had learned in my recent experiences, it was that nothing along this journey was insignificant. I noted the position of the symbols relative to each other, and once I was satisfied with my sketch, I dropped through the gap in the cave floor to return to Relto.

Return of the Bahro

The Return of the Fissure

Crack between Relto pedestals split and became a starry fissure once I returned the last Bahro Pillar.

As soon as I reappeared in Relto, the outline of the fissure shone brightly, and the entire island began to shake. With a brilliant flash of light, the ground in the middle of the fissure sunk into the earth— or, more precisely, into the starry expanse underneath it.

I couldn't even begin to imagine how it was possible, but it seemed as if there was a starry fissure that began just a dozen feet or so beneath the surface of the island! Or, perhaps Yeesha had managed to write this violation of the laws of physics into the Age somehow. She had certainly proven her ability to write just about anything she wanted thus far.

I couldn't keep myself calm enough to consider the origin of the fissure, however. Looking at its jagged edges reminded me of my first view of the Cleft, and a wave of homesickness crashed over me. Wherever this fissure led to, it marked the end of my journey. Perhaps now I could finally go home.

With one last backward glance at the humble hut that had served me so well during my journey, I stepped forward and fell through the fissure. After several unsettling seconds of free fall, I felt myself link away from Relto.

Prima's Official Travel Guide

As the link faded, I saw the desert come into view around me. Actually, it came into view below me—about fifteen feet below me! I tumbled out of the sky and landed near the ruins of Gehn's telescope, where I stood up and brushed the dust from my jeans. Once again, I'd survived a considerable fall without injury; I was either getting really good at taking them, or I had reserves of dumb luck I'd never known about.

Dropping through starry fissure returned me to the Cleft, near the telescope and Wahrk skeleton.

Judging from the telescope wreckage, the star fissure I'd just fallen through was the same one as the one in <u>Riven</u>, or at least connected to it in some way. Perhaps there was something about the shape of the fissure that somehow recalled the shape of the Cleft, where Gehn, Atrus, and Yeesha had all spent some time.

I was too tired to consider the metaphysics of star fissure linking. I just wanted to sleep for about a week. But sketching the symbols on the floor of the Bahro Cave and seeing how they were arranged made me think of the Imager in the Cleft.

Went to find Zandi, but he was no longer there.

I wondered if Yeesha had left a hidden message there for anyone who completed the journey she'd set before them. If there was nothing more to the journey, then that was fine. But if I didn't test my theory, I knew that I'd never be able to fall asleep, no matter how exhausted I was.

Before I entered the Cleft, I wanted to tell Zandi of my journey, but he wasn't there. I tried to figure out how long I had been gone (days? weeks?), but I couldn't even hazard a guess. It was then I realized that someone must have wondered about my disappearance. I hoped that the cops hadn't shown up with a warrant and hauled Zandi off! I resolved to enter Zandi's trailer and see if it had a phone— right after I checked out that Imager.

Entered Cleft laboratory to reach Imager.

Entered Bahro Cave floor symbols into Imager; Yeesha's image appeared w/ a new message & gifts for me.

I found the Cleft exactly as I'd left it. I crossed the suspension bridge that led to the kitchen, and from there, I went into the laboratory. I entered the symbols from the Bahro Cave floor into the Imager and pressed the blue button. Once again, the image of Yeesha appeared and spoke, but she had a new message for me:

"An ending has been written.

"You've done all that has been asked. You've traveled the full circle, you have returned to the Cleft, through the fissure, you swam among the stars and saw the remnants of previous journeys, you have returned, and the Pillars were returned, and now one more of the Bahro, the Least, has been returned to D'ni. You don't need to understand what that means, only that the hand of the Maker has set it in motion.

"Now the circle is complete and the tree has begun to grow again. The path is now open, and so the symbol of the journey must change. Now the beginning is tied to the end. Now you can go where you wish. The restoration of D'ni awaits—the deep city breathes. Uru again.

"And I will be concerned with other things. The Least are becoming greater. They will now also affect the restoration . . . perhaps not the way others had planned.

"You've learned about the pride of D'ni. The great Writers of worlds were infected with pride that became a cancer. It grew quietly beneath the surface, but it grew until D'ni could live no more.

"But those things have been told. You understand it well, I think. Let us end this cycle with rewards, before we start the next cycle.

"Relto—the high place—your Age now. It was the first Age I wrote—a gift for my parents—and now much more. It reminds me of another home, another place. I even placed the Library in the place it belongs. But Relto will change. It will be your soul, showing what you are. Only I could write Relto—it's beyond what the D'ni could accomplish. Keep it.

"And I've given you clothing that represents your journey. Wear this to show others what side you've taken, when sides are taken. When you wear it, you will tell all that you side with us, with Yeesha, with the Bahro. It will not always be easy.

"And another gift is 'here,' a link to the Cleft here in Tomahna. You haven't been able to return here, but now you can, this Book will take a special place on your shelf. This place is not meant to be shared. Return here alone when you wish to remember the cycle of things."

I took the Linking Book and placed my hand on the Linking Panel. I felt the sensation of the link, but when I reappeared, it seemed as if nothing had changed. It took me a second to realize that the Cleft was a bit darker, and instead of looking at a projection of Yeesha, I was now looking at Yeesha herself, in the flesh! I'd waited so long to speak to her, but now that I had my chance, I couldn't form a single word. Yeesha—the real Yeesha—continued to speak:

Touched the Linking Book Yeesha offered and linked to a darker Cleft with rain clouds outside— and the real Yeesha in the lab!

". . . Returning. . . . One final gift—something that no D'ni Writer has been able to do for more than 10,000 years. I alone can write this gift. I alone am chosen to do this . . . and more.

"This gift is what my father Atrus would have longed to give his grandmother Ti'ana . . . what Ti'ana longed for, and danced for . . . the gift of life in the desert."

The sudden flash of a bolt of lighting illuminated the Cleft walls for a split second, followed by the low roll of thunder. It was then that I realized why the Cleft seemed to be so dark; storm clouds were overhead, and the rain had begun to fall in the desert. Yeesha walked toward the door and looked back at me.

"Perhaps the ending has not yet been written."

And with that, she left the laboratory, the door closing behind her. I tried to follow, but by the time I opened the door and ran through it to meet her, she had already disappeared.

Epilogue

Final Yeesha Page

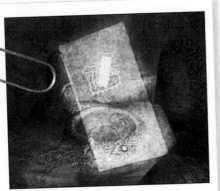

Final Yeesha Page was in the dish-shaped projector w/ the blinking green button near the lab door.

There was no way that Yeesha could have left the Cleft so quickly without linking away from it. I realized that there was no point in trying to find her if she didn't want to be found.

Instead, I turned to look at the one device in the laboratory that I'd never been able to operate successfully, the dish-shaped object with the blinking green button. I pressed the button, and the holographic image of the page I'd seen earlier appeared in front of me. This time, however, it didn't vanish. It flickered and rotated in front of me, and I realized that it was a final Yeesha Page. I reached out to touch it, and it added a page to my Linking Book that caused rain to fall in Relto.

Letter from Atrus

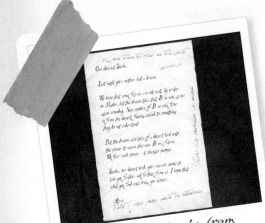

Reread letter to Yeesha from Atrus in the Cleft sleeping chamber; took on a whole new meaning now.

Exiting the laboratory, I investigated the rest of the Cleft. With the exception of the darkened skies and rain, it was the exact same Cleft as the one that began my journey. It was incredible that Yeesha could make such a major change to an existing Age without compromising the Age's stability. From what I knew of Writing, the D'ni were extremely reluctant to modify Ages once they were created, as doing so could set off a chain reaction of unintended consequences.

But, somehow, Yeesha had managed to pull it off. Everything was the same, right down to the letter from her father in the Cleft bedroom. I picked it up and read it again to see if its meaning had changed for me from the beginning of my journey:

Our dearest Yeesha,

Last night your mother had a dream. . . .

We know that some futures are not cast, by writer or Maker, but the dream tells that D'ni will grow again someday. New seekers of D'ni will flow in from the desert, feeling called to something they do not understand.

But the dream also tells of a desert bird with the power to weave this new D'ni's future. We fear such power—it changes people.

Yeesha, our desert bird, your search seems to take you further and further from us. I hope that what you find will bring you closer.

—Your Father, Atrus

My hands shook as I read the letter. Not only was it from the legendary Atrus himself, but I now saw through Atrus's careful diplomacy and could tell that he and Catherine were clearly critical of their daughter's efforts.

More chilling than Atrus's fears were the handwritten notes in its margins, which could have been written only by Yeesha: "I will use them to bring me the Least . . . Impossible . . . Now his burden is mine. . . . What I have found must be returned."

I felt the blood drain from my face. I'd been "used" to bring her the Least. What exactly had I done? And what did she mean by "his burden is mine?"

The Bahro

I climbed out of the Cleft to the surface, its baked brown soil already transforming into watery mud from the rain. As I stood and surveyed the desert, I heard an inhuman screech coming from the direction of the volcano. I'd heard that screech before—in the Bahro Caves.

I don't like judging anything by its appearance, but those Bahro made me nervous.

I turned and saw several humanoid figures along the lip of the volcano. So these were the Bahro. Even from a distance, there was something unsettling about their hunched shapes and the way they moved—more like insects than men. One by one, they descended into the smoking vent, seemingly unaffected by the intense heat.

The last one stopped at the volcano's summit and turned. I could have sworn that it looked straight at me as it raised its arms and unleashed a piercing scream. The Bahro then turned and joined its fellows inside the volcano.

Was that scream meant to be one of thanks or victory, or was it a war cry? Or was it all three?

Return to Relto

As miraculous as the rain was, the Cleft didn't feel like the one from which I'd started my journey. My Age, which I called Earth and Atrus's people had called D'ni, had a desert without a cloud in the sky. Yeesha had called this place Tomahna, a word that her mother had used to describe the Cleft, but I had the feeling that, contrary

Linked back to Relto and opened new, leftmost Linking Book in my Library—it had two Linking Panels to the Cleft.

to Yeesha's boasting, Anna would not have approved of it. I couldn't say for sure that it was my home, and I don't think that Anna would have been able to either.

I linked back to Relto. With the addition of the final Yeesha Page to my Linking Book, the rain pounded down on the island, which did nothing to improve my mood.

I entered my hut and looked at my Library, which now had a new book at the far left of the shelf. I picked up the book and opened it. Inside were two Linking Panels, one showing the rainy Cleft and one showing the sunny Cleft.

I shut the book and slumped against the wall of the hut as the endless rain beat a merciless tattoo on the rocky soil outside.

Yeesha had used me; that much was clear now. She had rationed out information, never telling me the whole story, never giving me a chance to weigh the facts and decide for myself if her journey was one worth taking. The Ages she showed me were carefully selected to support her point of view that D'ni was a proud and exploitative Age. I had let my natural curiosity get the better of me, focusing on solving her riddles and puzzles without taking a moment to understand the consequences of doing so. And during those times when I thought that the journey wasn't worth it, there was always the threat of never being able to return home if I didn't see it through.

Yeesha made the journey sound as if it was only a tour through the less well-known chapters of D'ni history, when in actuality she was using me to bring a Bahro back to D'ni. I didn't even know where I was bringing it back <u>from</u> or how it wound up there. If it was trapped, then why couldn't Yeesha release it? If it was locked away, then why was it locked away? Was this an attempt to convince me to join her "side," the side of the Bahro? And if so, who made up the other side?

Maybe Yeesha was right to use me to do her dirty work. Maybe if I'd known all of the facts, I would have concluded that Yeesha acted out of the best of intentions. But everyone knows what the road to Hell is paved with, and if there was a more demonic sight than those Bahro descending into the molten throat of the volcano, I couldn't imagine it.

<u>Those</u> Bahro. I saw more than one on the volcano. And yet, Yeesha said I'd released only one. I obviously wasn't the first person Yeesha had used to free a Bahro, and I had a feeling I wouldn't be the last. How many other explorers had embarked on the journey that Yeesha set before them, and how many had seen it through to the end and released a Bahro into D'ni?

And aside from the fact that I resented being exploited, I was starting to see inconsistencies in Yeesha's logic. She had accused the D'ni of falling victim to their own pride, but how proud had she sounded in her final speech?

"You don't need to understand what that means, only that the hand of the Maker has set it in motion."

"Only I could write Relto—it's beyond what the D'ni could accomplish."

"I alone can write this gift. I alone am chosen to do this . . . and more."

When she spoke like that, she sounded more like her grandfather than her parents. I had read in <u>The Book of Atrus</u> how Gehn had tried to correct a problem in one of his Ages and made changes so drastic that his Linking Book wound up taking him to a different Age that was almost identical to the one it had originally linked to. It was from Gehn's mistakes that Atrus learned to exercise caution and humility.

I stood back up and opened the Linking Book with the two Cleft panels.

There was still too much I didn't know about what was happening, and I needed to get some answers. Yeesha may have held the DRC in contempt, and while I had to admit that they did seem a little too bureaucratic and officious, there was no doubt that they knew a lot more about D'ni than I did.

I would find Dr. Watson, I decided as I placed my hand on the book's right Linking Panel. I would join the DRC and hear what they had to say about Yeesha and the Bahro. The link brought me back to the desert where my journey had begun. I had come full circle.

Yeesha's great-grandmother, Anna, had been taught by her father to develop total awareness of her surroundings. I read in <u>The Book of Ti'ana</u> how he would ask her the same question repeatedly: "What do you see?"

It was a mantra designed to teach her that nothing was insignificant, and that sound decisions were based on careful observations. Just as Anna's father passed the mantra down to her, so did she pass it down to her grandson, Atrus.

Time to go and find Dr. Watson and the DRC; there's more going on here than I can fathom alone.

And standing there in the desert, I imagined three generations of explorers who had come there before me asking the same question:

<u>What do you see?</u>

I looked back at Zandi's trailer and the Cleft. And then I saw the smoking crater of the volcano and remembered the scream of the Bahro.

"I see trouble brewing," I said to myself as I pushed open the gate and started my long hike back toward civilization.

Appendix A
Explorer's Reference

Publisher's Note

In exchange for allowing us to reprint DRC research journals found by the author during his journey, the DRC was given access to the journals of the author. We offer this bullet-point explorer's reference as a document of future historical importance and as a reference to any amateur explorers who wish to retrace the author's steps.

While this explorer's reference will get you from the start of Yeesha's journey to the end of it, it is intended to do so as quickly as possible. That means that it does not mention optional detours or areas of interest—such as Yeesha Pages, non-essential Linking Stones, or DRC journals found along the way. Refer to the author's narrative in the previous chapters for a more detailed view of the journey.

Cleft

Outside the Cleft

— Touch Journey Cloth #1 on the back of the "No Trespassing" sign.

— Touch Journey Cloth #2 on the back of Zandi's trailer.

— Touch Journey Cloth #3 on the inside of the Wahrk skeleton.

— Enter the Cleft via the ladder.

Cross the Cleft

— Walk across the bridge that leads to the unlocked door; bridge snaps.

— Climb the bridge "ladder" to a sleeping chamber.

— Touch Journey Cloth #4 on the wall of the sleeping chamber.

— Cross the plank bridge to the other side of the Cleft.

— Climb up the bridge "ladder" to the laboratory's open door.

Power the Cleft and View Imager

- Release the windmill brake in the kitchen.

- Return to the surface and push the handle on the windmill to start it turning.

- Return to the laboratory and enter the symbols near the door into the Imager.

- Activate the Imager and listen to Yeesha's speech.

- Touch Journey Cloth #5, revealed by Yeesha, in the laboratory.

Touch Remaining Journey Cloths

- Close the laboratory door.

- Exit through the kitchen door and cross the bridge beyond it.

- Touch Journey Cloth #6, hanging on the outside of the laboratory door.

- Step on the foot pedal in front of the bucket winch to lower the bucket.

- Touch Journey Cloth #7 on the side of the lowered bucket.

Open Bahro Door and link to Relto

- After finding all seven Journey Cloths, touch the Bahro Door at the base of the tree in the Cleft to open it.

- Descend the ladder and follow the pathway to a Linking Book.

- Use the Book to link to Relto.

Teledahn

Link to Teledahn from Relto

- Standing with your back to the Relto hut, touch the hand icon on the near-right pedestal to reveal the Teledahn Linking Book.

— Touch the Linking Panel to link to Teledahn.

— Upon appearing in the hut in Teledahn, walk around the exterior of the hut to find and touch Journey Cloth #1.

Restore Power

— Exit the hut and follow the pathway to the power tower, bearing left at the only fork in the path.

— Pump the priming switch three times to raise the tower.

— Line up the sun in the center of the viewfinder and set the viewfinder rotating counterclockwise so that the sun remains in the center of it; power is restored.

— Pull all three levers near the power tower. Two activate giant camshafts; the third is broken.

Bucket Ride to Control Room

— Pull lever next to bucket loader to start the countdown.

— Quickly jump into the bucket to ride to the control room.

— If you miss the bucket, pull the lever again to stop the buckets and start over.

Control Room

— Touch Journey Cloth #2 hanging on the wall of the control room.

— Use the control panel to drain the water below the hut and unlock the hatch in the hut where you started.

— Step on the foot brake in front of the elevator to release it.

— Press the blue button in the elevator to ride up to the Teledahn office.

Teledahn Office

— Touch Journey Cloth #3 on the office wall.

— Make a note of the pressure plate diagram on the desk.

— Review other materials as you see fit (optional).

— Return to the elevator and press the green button twice to return to the hut where you started.

Slave Caverns

- Open the hatch in the hut's floor and climb down the ladders into the storm drain.

- Exit the storm drain through a crack in its side to reach the slave caverns.

- Touch Journey Cloth #4 on the wall of the slave caverns.

- Move rocks or large bones onto the four pressure plates closest to the two locked gates to open the gates.

- Proceed into the next chamber; flip any of the switches on the wall to close the gate you just came through and open the exit gate.

Outside Slave Caverns

- Walk down the pathway past the slave caverns until you reach a raised section of the path.

- Jump directly at the raised pathway to loosen it, then pull the lever in front of it to lower it.

- Continue along the path to a plateau.

- Jump up the crates near the door to reach a ledge containing Journey Cloth #5; touch the Journey Cloth.

- Enter the door near the crates.

Mining Gun

- Proceed along the metal pathway through a door and into a cavern.

- Touch Journey Cloth #6 on the cavern's wall.

- Proceed down the tunnel and subsequent pathway next to Journey Cloth #6 to find a mining gun.

- Use the mining gun to shatter hanging boulders in the distances; one of them is the counterweight for a hanging ladder near Journey Cloth #5.

Climbing the Ladder

— Return to the ledge where you found Journey Cloth #5.

— Climb the ladder you just lowered to reach a room with Journey Cloth #7 in it.

— Descend the stairs to reach a secret door leading back to the room downstairs.

— From that room, proceed up the metal pathway and into the cavern beyond it to find the Bahro Door near Journey Cloth #6.

Bahro Cave

— After finding and touching all seven Journey Cloths, touch the Bahro Door to open it.

— Proceed through it to link to the Bahro Cave.

— Touch the hand icon on the wall to remove the Bahro Pillar to Relto.

— Drop into the starry void below the cave to link back to Relto.

Gahreesen

Link to Gahreesen

— Standing with your back to the Relto hut, touch the hand icon on the far-left pedestal to reveal the Linking Book to Gahreesen.

— Use the Book to link into Gahreesen.

Retrieve Your KI

— From the link-in point, follow the path to the KI Dispenser.

— Activate the KI Dispenser to get your KI.

To the Second Floor

— Proceed past the safety cones into the next room.

— Leap the gap in the floor and look for Journey Cloth #1 in the rubble beyond it.

— Enter the beetle cages through the crack in the wall.

— Climb up on one set of cages to reach Journey Cloth #2.

— Climb up the other set of cages and jump up the rubble to reach the second floor.

To the Gear Room

— Walk into the "rotating" wall through the crack in the hall wall.

— Walk into the Gear Room from the "rotating" wall through another crack in the wall.

— Touch Journey Cloth #3 on the wall of the Gear Room.

Restoring the Power

— Stand on the primer pump pressure plate until the pump is at full pressure.

— Run to the leftmost switch on the bank of switches and activate it; return to the pressure plate before the pump loses its pressure.

— Repressurize the pump, then step on the far foot switch next to the giant gear. Return to the primer pump to repressurize it.

— Step on the near foot switch next to the giant gear. Return to the primer pump to repressurize it.

— Run to the second switch from the left (marked with a gear icon) and activate it to restore power to the gear.

— Flip the two remaining unlit switches to restore power to the elevator and doors.

To the Roof

— Return to the first floor via the same route you use to reach the second floor.

— Ride the elevator in the first floor hallway (across from the KI Dispenser) to reach the roof.

Training Facility

— Jump from the extended walkway on the roof to the highest pinnacle between the two rotating buildings.

— Touch Journey Cloth #4, hanging on the side of this pinnacle.

— Jump from the pinnacle to any of the six pathways extending from the Training Facility.

— Run to the pathway's end to enter the Training Facility.

- Head to the Conference Room in the Training Center that has Journey Cloth #5 hanging on the wall.

Gahreesen Prison

- Link back to Relto, then link to Teledahn.
- Use the Linking Stone in the room near the Bahro Door to link into a Gahreesen prison cell.
- Touch Journey Cloth #6 on the wall of the cell.
- Drop through the hatch in the cell to reach the hallways below.
- Walk away from the barred window overlooking the outside of the prison.
- At the first four-way intersection, turn right.
- At the next four-way intersection, go straight.
- At the third four-way intersection, turn left and climb the ladder at the hall's end.
- Enter the door at the ladder's top to enter the Training Room.
- Climb either ladder extending through the ceiling of the training room.
- Find Journey Cloth #7 on one of the outer support pillars at the top of the ladders.
- Link back to Relto, and then link back to Gahreesen.

Bahro Cave

- Return to the pinnacle between the two rotating buildings.
- Jump to the nearby pinnacle that isn't quite as tall.
- From there, leap to the ledge with the Bahro Door on it.
- After finding and activating all seven Journey Cloths, touch the Bahro Door and proceed through it to link to the Bahro Cave.
- Touch the hand icon on the wall to remove the Bahro Pillar to Relto.
- Drop into the starry void to link back to Relto.

Prima's Official Travel Guide

Kadish Tolesa

Link to Kadish Tolesa

– With your back to the Relto hut, touch the hand icon on the far-right pedestal to reveal the Kadish Tolesa Linking Book.

– Use the Book to link to Kadish Tolesa.

Kadish Tolesa Gallery

– From the link-in point, face the giant tree behind you and follow the left-hand path to a ruined courtyard.

– Follow the edge of the courtyard in a clockwise direction to reach Journey Cloth #1.

– Use the Linking Book in the gazebo in the middle of the courtyard to link to the Kadish Tolesa Gallery.

– All five of the major artworks near the Linking Book in the Gallery are clues to the puzzles you must solve; make a note of them.

– Use the Linking Book in the Gallery to return to the gazebo from which you linked.

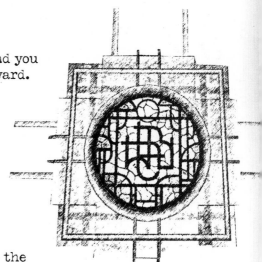

Ring Pattern Alignment

– Look through the alignment device near the Gallery Linking Book.

– Align the three rings with the alignment device so that they match the top image in the Gallery triptych.

– Return to your link-in point and take the right-hand path, making a left at the only intersection in the path.

– Find Journey Cloth #2 on the side of the raised platform that holds the second alignment device.

– Use the second alignment device to align the next set of rings so that they match the middle image in the Gallery triptych.

– Walk down the pedestal stairs and continue walking in a straight line to reach the third alignment device.

- Use the third alignment device to align the final set of rings so that they match the bottom image in the Gallery triptych.

- This opens a door in a nearby tree. Proceed through the door.

Shadow Path

- On the other side of the door is a blue switch. Press it to close the door and reveal Journey Cloth #3.

- Walk down the spiral staircases. Press the second, third, and fifth glowing blue switches, which casts a pattern of light and shadow on the floor.

- Walk along the shadow path to the room's center to reveal a hidden passage. Go through the door at the end.

Glowing Symbol Path

- Follow the path to reach a vista and a ziggurat.

- Find Journey Cloth #4 in an exterior alcove of the ziggurat.

- Enter the ziggurat and press the glowing blue switch to shine light onto the floor.

- Press the switch again after a minute to shut off the light. The floor now glows with blue symbols.

- Walk on only the tiles that show a variation of the Kadish Tolesa tree symbol as seen in the Gallery.

- When you reach the last tile, it becomes an elevator and descends through the floor.

Pillars

- Touch Journey Cloth #5 in the hall that leads to the pillars.

- The leftmost lever in the pillar room controls the nearest pillar, the rightmost lever in the pillar room controls the farthest pillar, etc.

- Raise the second pillar once, the third pillar three times, and the fourth pillar four times.

- Climb the pillars to reach an alcove with Journey Cloth #6.

- Descend the alcove stairs to return to the levers. Press the blue button to reset the pillars.

- Raise the first pillar once, the second pillar four times, the third pillar once, and the fourth pillar twice to drop a ladder from the ceiling.

- Climb up the second pillar to reach the ladder. Climb the ladder.

Vault

- Follow the pathway to the control panel for the vault.

- Press the buttons in this order: 1-5-2-3-4-6.

- Enter the vault and jump up the piles of treasure opposite the door to reach Journey Cloth #7.

Bahro Cave

- Return to the vault control panel and drop onto the huge guy wire that stretches over the Bahro Door ledge.

- Leap from the guy wire to the ledge, and touch the Bahro Door to open it (assuming you have touched all seven Journey Cloths).

- Go through the Bahro Door to link to the Bahro Cave.

- Touch the hand icon to remove the Bahro Pillar to Relto.

- Drop into the starry abyss to return to Relto.

Eder Gira and Eder Kemo

Link to Upper Gira

- With your back to the Relto hut, touch the hand icon on the near left pedestal to reveal the Eder Gira Linking Book.

- Use the Book to link to Upper Gira.

Upper Gira

— Drop onto the small ledge that overlooks the lava river to reach Journey Cloth #1.

— Run from that ledge onto the pinnacle in the lava river's center, and step on the fumarole foot switch to close the fumarole.

— Leap from that pinnacle to the nearby plateau; if you miss, you will "panic-link" to Relto, so don't worry.

— Close the two fumaroles on that plateau.

— Cross the land bridge and close the fumarole at the end.

— There is a ledge above one of the two open fumaroles. Close the fumarole that is <u>not</u> directly below the ledge.

— Stand on the fumarole beneath the ledge to shoot up to the ledge and touch Journey Cloth #2.

— Drop off that ledge and go to the other side of Upper Gira. Open the fumarole directly in front of a short rock wall.

— Return to the other open fumarole and close it.

— Return to the open fumarole and stand on it to shoot over the rock wall.

— Follow the path to Lower Gira.

Lower Gira, Part 1

— Jump into the cavern beyond the twin waterfalls.

— Turn on both torches in the cavern.

— Push the hexagonal basket out of the cavern and into the water.

— Maneuver the hexagonal basket so that it rests squarely in the narrow brook between the cavern and the shrine with the Linking Book in it.

— Use the Linking Book in the shrine to link to Eder Kemo.

Eder Kemo

— Touch Journey Cloth #3, which is hanging on the back side of the largest stone pillar in the courtyard rock garden.

— Touch Journey Cloth #4, which is hanging on a rock wall in the bamboo grove.

— Touch Journey Cloth #5, which is hanging on a lamppost that overlooks a stone rest area near the "brain trees."

- Touch Journey Cloth #6, which is hanging on a rock wall in the puffer grove.

- Wait for the rain to start and stop, then walk through the cloud of glow bugs near the brain trees to attract them. Running, jumping, or exposing the bugs to water will cause them to flee.

- Walk down the path, past the puffer grove, until you reach a Linking Book; use it to link back to Lower Gira.

Lower Gira, Part 2

- Walk around the steam vent directly in front of you, and walk over the basket you placed in the stream.

- Jump into the cavern behind the waterfall without landing in the water; you will lose only half of your glow bugs.

- Walk through the dark tunnel in the cavern.

- Light the torch at the cavern's end.

- Open the wooden door in the cavern to reveal another tunnel.

- Go through this tunnel until you reach the top of the twin waterfalls.

- Walk through the water to find another cavern with two more hexagonal baskets (you will lose your glow bugs).

- Push both hexagonal baskets off of the top of the waterfalls so that they land in front of the lower cavern.

- Return to the lower cavern and push the two baskets into position between the cavern entrance and the shore so that you can enter the cavern without jumping or walking through water.

- Return to Eder Kemo and get more glow bugs, then link back to Eder Gira.

- Walk across all three hexagonal baskets and into the cavern behind the waterfalls; you shouldn't lose any glow bugs.

- Proceed through the darkened tunnel and turn left at the end to ascend another darkened tunnel that ends in a narrow outdoor ledge.

- Walk along the ledge and jump the gap; you will lose half of your glow bugs.

- Continue to the end of the ledge and enter the cavern.

- Turn on the torch in the cavern.

— Touch Journey Cloth #7, which hangs on the wall of the cavern.

— Return to the Linking Book shrine and link to Eder Kemo.

Bahro Cave

— Follow the Eder Kemo path to the Bahro Door.

— After activating all seven Journey Cloths, touch the Bahro Door to open it.

— Proceed through the door to link to the Bahro Cave.

— Touch the hand icon on the wall to remove the final Bahro Pillar to Relto.

— Drop into the starry void to link back to Relto.

End of the Journey

Returning the Pillars

— Revisit each Age (Teledahn, Gahreesen, Kadish Tolesa, and Eder Kemo) and reenter each Bahro Cave through the Age's Bahro Door.

— Touch the hand icon to return the Age's Bahro Pillar to the Bahro Cave.

> **NOTE**
> The following information is provided for research purposes only! DRC researchers are expressly forbidden from moving the Bahro Pillars from Relto back to the Bahro Cave until we understand more completely the effects and consequences of doing so!

— When you return all four Bahro Pillars, make a note of the four symbols on the floor of the Bahro Cave and their position relative to each other.

— Link back to Relto, where the star fissure opens between the pedestals.

Meeting Yeesha

— Drop through the star fissure to link back to the Cleft.

— Return to the laboratory and input the Bahro Cave symbols into the Imager; activate the Imager.

— Yeesha appears with gifts and a Linking Book to Tomahna.

— Use the Linking Book to link to Tomahna.

— Exit the Tomahna Cleft to see the Bahro enter the volcano—end of journey.

Appendix B: DRC Research

Found during Teledahn Journey

Note: From Marie to Dr. Watson

Dr. Watson—

Big problems. The house of Noloben is _not_ empty. I met someone there today. My D'ni isn't great, but I spoke with him for a while. Yeah, he's D'ni and, as we figured, he knows a lot about the creatures. _A whole lot._

We obviously need a meeting AS AP.

—Marie

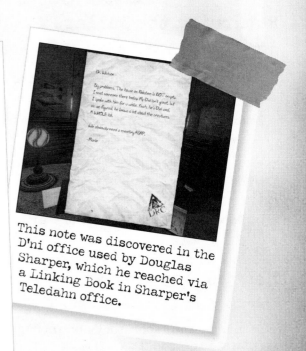

This note was discovered in the D'ni office used by Douglas Sharper, which he reached via a Linking Book in Sharper's Teledahn office.

Journal: Douglas Sharper (Personal)

11.14.97—Looks like they've agreed to let me take control of Teledahn. Time to start a journal. Officially.

11.17.97—Maybe not. Kodama popped in, going on about his inspections, in his usual arrogant manner. What a joke.

11.24.97—Now it's Watson's turn. Acted as though he was chatting but I could tell he was looking all over, checking on my progress, or maybe making sure I can be trusted. I'll just get used to it.

This journal was discovered in the D'ni office used by Douglas Sharper, which he reached via a Linking Book in Sharper's Teledahn office.

11.25.97—Time to move forward. DRC isn't going to change anytime soon.

12.15.97—Merry Christmas. Going up for a few months. Can't take this red tape anymore.

1.29.98—Yay for Broncos. Patriots should have been there. Stupid Steelers. Okay, maybe Teledahn will help me to forget all this.

2.15.98—Looks like I'm going to need Watson after all. I've found all kinds of journals and notes upstairs that I'm going to need translated. I think Watson is going to let one of his assistants help me out. Sam.

3.1.98—Sam is not the fastest translator I've ever seen. I don't think he's even started. Kodama came by again today.

3.3.98—Spotted something today. Creature of some kind. Forget the history of this place, for now. I've got to see that thing again.

3.7.98—Saw her again. Wow. What a beauty.

3.9.98—She's very sensitive to sound. Startles like an antelope. I'm estimating she's a good forty feet. Killer-whale type. Hard shell though.

3.18.98—No sign of her in this area, at least. Sam said he's going to have some time next week. At this rate. . . .

3.25.98—She showed up again. I saw her eating. She likes the Flappers. Feeds on them. Pretty quick and agile for her size. Surprised me. Of course, those Flappers aren't real bright. Those who weren't eaten went right back to the spot and waited for her to show up again.

Looks like this place was written in 8990 for a D'ni Lord. Guild of Caterers. 250th birthday present. If I'm ever 250, someone better give me something better than this place.

4.5.98—Sam is busy again. Did get me some more translations though. Seems like the mushrooms were used for some kind of delicacy. To be honest, I'm not sure Sam got that one right. Doesn't make a lot of sense, not with what I'm seeing.

4.7.98—Watson told me Sam is too busy to help me. I'm going to have to learn this language myself, or find someone who can actually help me.

4.8.98—Watched her for a while today. Definitely feeds on the Flappers close to shore. Also feeds on mushrooms.

4.15.98—Does she ever feed on mushrooms. Watched her completely destroy one today. Brought the whole thing down and fed for some time. Until scared off by something.

4.17.98—Mushroom is gone. Probably sank. Kodama came by again today and I was glad the girl wasn't around. Last thing I need.

5.14.98—1. The Flappers like the spores. 2. The creature likes the Flappers. 3. She's scared to death of loud sounds. If I get this equipment running, she's gone. Heading up in a week. Going to try and get this gate down before I go. See if she'll come in while I'm gone.

5.20.98—Gate is down. See what happens when I come back. Hopefully there are mushrooms left.

8.12.98—Three mushrooms were down. Seems all of them were a particular kind. She was in the lagoon. I think I could have taken her out, but not yet. DRC would have a fit. Probably kick me out or something. She's definitely an air breather. Could hear her today. Sleeping, on the surface. Kodama followed me here and scared the heck out of her. She woke and shot out of here, fast. Kodama never saw her. Apparently some new guy is learning D'ni and wants to work with me. We'll see.

8.28.98—There are quite a few new people coming down. A group from some game company
was recently here and there was quite a stir. I met a few of them.
Nice guys.

9.15.98—Haven't seen her for a full month. I'm going to start working on the equipment
here. Can't wait forever and the DRC is getting on me. As though they owned
the place.

10.1.98—The tower is almost working. Need some tools from the surface. No sign of
Shroomie. Met the new guy—Nick—nice guy. This might be real good. Smart guy.
Picking up D'ni fast. He's going to keep at it, but I gave him some material to
study in the meantime.

11.5.98—Quick trip up and back down. Tower is working. Nick dropped off some
translation and it all matches the old stuff. He's working on new material
now. Tower is power and more projects.

11.14.98—These buckets are a mess. So is the elevator. Have found some kind of pump
mechanism to get that water out. I think all of it will have to wait. I'm
heading back up for holidays and end of season. Tickets to Monday night game
against Miami. Patriots still in the playoff hunt.

1.7.99—Patriots out. Back down. Nick is more than I could have hoped for. Seems up for
keeping the translation out of DRC's hands. Has had some bad experiences
with Kodama and Engberg and in my camp now. Perfect.

Apparently Hinahsh only owned the Age for ten years. At his death, Teledahn
was left to the Guild of Caterers who installed the equipment that I'm working
on today. Some of the translation has actually been rather helpful. I think I
can get the pump working. Was never meant for water, but I think it would pump
out the water.

Nick says there is quite a bit about a Guild Captain Ventus who ran the Age for
quite a few years and directed the industrialization of the place. Did quite a
job apparently. Although, Nick is still reading.

Signs of Shroomie, but I haven't seen her for a long time and I'm not going to
stop working on the equipment now. Apparently no mention of her in the stuff
Nick is reading.

2.4.99—Pump works, although I'm keeping the water there. Nice form of protection to the
other side. At least until I discover what it was used for. That's Nick's job now.
I have my ideas though.

Seems as though Ventus installed the gate to keep Shroomie out of here.
Didn't like her eating his mushrooms. Good idea.

2.6.99—Ventus maybe wasn't so great after all. Ruined the place. Turned it into what we see now. Explains the differences in early descriptions to the later ones.

Seems the Age was auctioned off and that's all of the official records. Nick can share those with the DRC. I don't mind.

2.8.99—Showed Nick some of the manuscripts I've kept hidden. I'm quite sure I can trust him. He's given the official report to Watson and the others and is willing to do these extra translations on the side. Good man.

3.1.99—Watson, Kodama, and Sutherland came by today. It was pre-arranged so they didn't see anything they didn't need to. They seem satisfied with the work I'm doing, although the fact they continue to check on me still drives me mad. They say they want the Age ready for visitors relatively soon. I didn't realize that anyone and everyone would be allowed access to the place but why not I suppose. I'll still have my areas.

3.4.99—Big argument today with Watson. Upset I didn't share with him all that Nick had translated. Miscommunication, although I'm happy Nick has kept his mouth closed regarding the other. Regardless, I can't take their nit-picking. I'm heading to the surface for a long trip. Returning to Africa again with the fellows. Don't know when I'll be back here.

Nick knows to keep things quiet. I've set things up for Shroomie to return and I have plans to bring down some new items. Look forward to returning a long time from now.

2.15.00—Back to Teledahn again. The surface trip triggered some ideas for here that I think I'll begin exploring. Some talks with Engberg might be in order soon.

Nick has gotten a load of translation done. I'm going to try and summarize as best I can. If I can remember everything.

This place was owned by a fellow named Manesmo. The man apparently got the place cheap somewhere. He started the harvesting of spores again—it seems the Age had corrected itself over time. Bread apparently, they were making. The same delicacy D'ni had raved about before. Made a decent amount of money.

However, he was doing lots of stuff in the dark. Slave trading. I'm sure Watson would have a fit if he knew this. His precious D'ni. Where they were going, we can't find out. But it explains the cages and the whole backside of this place, really. Hiding from Maintainers I suppose.

We found some more mention of Shroomie as well. Manesmo saw her pretty frequently. They even found her nest. I'm heading out tomorrow to see.

As far as Shroomie herself, she has been here, but was not here when I arrived. Shrooms have managed to disappear and she broke a walkway on the backside. Have to fix that now.

2.17.00—No nest. Remains, yes, but she's obviously not been there for a long time. This place is much bigger than I thought. Learned that today.

3.3.00—The DRC is getting pretty serious about letting people down here. They have moved to The Island and are trying to get portions of the city open for visitors. Moving headquarters to a building there as well. I suppose I'm going to have to get serious about it as well. They're going to make me if I don't. So back to the equipment.

4.15.00—Cars are giving me all kinds of trouble. So is this ridiculous elevator and I don't know why. I'm making a quick trip to the surface. Parts.

5.23.00—Back with parts. Nick has found out that slaves were going to a place called Rebek. Haven't heard of it myself. I'm going to ask Watson tomorrow.

5.25.00—Watson has heard of it. Says they've been there. Asked how I knew and I realized it was a mistake to ask about it. Told him Nick told me and fortunately Nick told me later he had been doing some official translation for the Age. Lucky me. Be more careful.

5.28.00—Found a new book today. A very special book.

6.15.00—Cars are working. Why they need to work I don't know but apparently the DRC wants this place restored to its original condition. So, cars are working.

7.2.00—Elevators work. Finally. Nick tells me this Rebek Age was amazing but he was pulled off of it. Games with the slaves from here were played there. Hunting game of sorts. I'm not for hunting people but the game does sound fun. Doubt Watson will want to approve that Age too fast.

8.2.00—DRC is planning on opening this place up in 2002. They, of course, haven't bothered to tell me that but regardless, it's true. Working on getting some lights going in here. I have a feeling inspections will be increasing.

8.10.00—Watson informed me of the plans today. 2002 is the target. Thanks.

8.12.00—Nick stopped by and we've got a little more information. Looks like there is some kind of weapon in our hands. At least it could be used as a weapon. After the lights.

8.15.00—Inspection planned for next month.

9.12.00—Lights are functioning. Cars. Doors. Elevators. Not sure what else they'll want but I'm sure they'll come up with something.

9.15.00—Well, stupid me. I have an entire list of items that need to be accomplished for this place to be safe. I won't be taking any more Ages, after this one. Maybe a city location. I can't take this.

9.17.00—Shroomie is back. Watched her all day. Out of the blue, I think she's starting to like me. This could be good. I'll give up working for a short while.

9.20.00—She's nervous but coming back daily. I keep the gate down.

9.21.00—She's trapped. Got the gate up with her inside eating Flappers. Set her off. Pretty obvious she can be a nasty girl if she wants. But still I'll have a shot. And I need to do it before Kodama shows up.

9.22.00—Got her. Time for a surface trip with the important parts. I'll sink the rest.

10.30.00—Wooden walkways are fixed. Rails are up. Among the other things on the list of DRC requests. If this place isn't safe, I don't know what is. Inspection tomorrow.

Nick has dropped off some more translations. Seems as though a major inspection into the illegal activities was going on immediately before the fall. Doesn't look like they found anything.

11.1.00—Inspection went fine. I guess this place is safe now. I'm heading back to the surface for more tools, football, and the holidays.

2.1.01—Another missed playoffs. Oh well. Things are stressful here. One year to go for initial visitors and it is beginning to show. However, Sutherland dropped by today. Nice woman. We had a nice talk.

2.5.01—I'm helping out in the city now, not much work to do in Teledahn. Clean-up here and there. Maintain. I'm hoping for a certain location in the city, maybe my helping will get me some leverage with Watson. I'm enjoying the time with Sutherland anyway.

3.3.01—More city work. Not much happening here.

4.7.01—Nick managed to get me an extra Teledahn book today. Good man.

5.12.01—Shroomie is back! Obviously not the same one, but we've got a new girl here. Amazing. I'm curious to know how many there are now. I think I'm going to try and schedule another trip in the next couple of months.

5.23.01—The trip was a success. Amazing. There are quite a few of these creatures all over. Perhaps a seasonal thing. Waters where I had been before I found a pod of the creatures. And a bigger one. I'm not sure but these seem to be young ones. The larger creature was absolutely stunning. I've never seen anything like it in all my days of hunting. I was actually a little frightened. This thing could have swallowed my boat whole. To take even a small portion home would be . . . I'm going to have to think this one through.

6.1.01—Back to work here. I'm installing a gun of some kind down on the docks. It's a D'ni mining instrument I believe. Regardless, the DRC, of all people, want it set up. Strange.

6.30.01—Gun is up. Not working, but up. Laxman will have to get it working, or least give it a shot. Not familiar enough with this kind of D'ni technology.

7.5.01—More city work and less Teledahn work. Did clean up the cages and the larger mushroom. Took out some crates and moved them upstairs. I think another surface trip is in order. Marie wants to go up as well.

10.12.01—A little longer than I had expected for obvious reasons. Horrible tragedy. I'm happy to have D'ni. A distraction of sorts.

10.14.01—I brought down a fish tank. At least the first part. Want to see if I can learn more about these Flappers. I can get some young ones and some water from the lake. We'll see.

10.21.01—The stress level is rising rapidly. Only a few months out and they are planning on bringing down some visitors. They are cleaning up a neighborhood for a group of new people. Interesting.

11.2.01—Victor found some kind of communication device this week. A KI they are calling it. Very interesting device, I have to admit. Victor does seem to know his stuff, at least. Talked to Engberg about a building in the city that I'd like to have. We'll see.

11.3.01—Victor can't get to the gun for a long time. In fact, DRC wants the whole thing taken out now. Fine by me.

11.5.01—Found another new book today. Perhaps I have my city location now. Great view as well. I'm moving some things there. A little more out of the way. Glad I bought the more expensive fish tank now.

11.22.01—Received a report from the surface. Patriots aren't doing well and I don't think I'm going home this holiday. I'll help here. Teledahn seems stable but Kodama has asked me to look at a different Age and help them out. Sounds like an interesting place. Ahnonay or something. Why not?

12.12.01—Strange place. Needs lots of work but it's been good. I think I'm heading up to the surface. Watson had recommended we go up. Marie is joining me again.

2.10.02—Wasn't supposed to be gone this long but who would have thought the Patriots would win the Super Bowl! I don't think Watson is very pleased but too bad. Visitors are down and I wasn't here to see them.

2.16.02—The DRC wants me to go through Teledahn again, although I'm not sure why. This place has been cleaned up for months. Typical of them. I should know better by now.

2.17.02—New Shroomie creature seems pretty happy here. Runs when the machinery comes on but usually returns. I usually leave the gate down.

2.23.02—KIs are working great. Pretty amazing devices. Haven't met any new visitors. Watson says he doesn't want me to. Typical bureaucratic nonsense.

3.1.02—They are ready to open up The Island. I have to admit I'm pretty excited about watching these people visit. I'd love for them to come to Teledahn, but the DRC insists it's not ready. Not sure what more they want.

3.20.02—A new group of visitors are coming. The DRC is really hyping this one. Authorized explorers.

3.27.02—Enjoyed talking to Robyn and Rand again. Nice guys. Hadn't seen them in a long time. The new authorized explorers seem to be enjoying themselves. Fun.

4.5.02—Funny. DRC posts that restoration efforts will be given top priority this month. More meetings and more inspections when the Age has been ready for months. If it makes them feel better. They did acknowledge that I found the book. Wasn't expecting that.

On an even funnier note, all meetings are being held in the Tokotah now. I couldn't have asked for much more.

4.20.02—So they made that public! Shroomie was in here and I had to make up some reason to postpone the trip. If they had seen the equipment and such, in fact, it's time to get rid of some of this. If the DRC had come here today, could have been bad.

4.25.02—Phase Five approval. What's that even mean?

5.12.02—Simpson told me about a pretty strange stone, so I tried it out. I want it myself. I think I'll keep it here. Don't really care what the DRC thinks of that either.

5.17.02—Stone is gone. Vanished right out of my office. Where's Simpson?

5.20.02—Got the stone back again. Simpson claims it was back where he found it. Regardless, this time I'm keeping it in a more secure location.

5.25.02—Now Phase Five approval. I've been so angry this past month, I've been ready to throw in the towel and head back up. It's utterly ridiculous what they are doing. The safety requirements they are pulling out. Somebody had better do something before we have an all-out government down here. Although these threads on the forums may be something. The DRC, in secret, is suspecting Zandi. This could get fun.

Stone is gone again. How?

5.30.02—Last time with the stone. I'm trying a more secure location.

6.3.02—Gone again.

6.7.02—I have the stone more one time. Simpson says he can't take it again. So I'm trying one more thing. Gut feeling about these creatures.

6.18.02—Watching people here has been fun. Maybe it all has been worth it.

6.20.02—Stone hasn't gone anywhere this time. I think they're afraid of the hanging rocks. Interesting.

7.11.02—Surprise, Rebek was shelved. I saw this one months ago.

7.23.02—This is wild. They are flipping out over there with these Zandi breaches. Hilarious. I love it. Of course they haven't mentioned a thing to me yet. I'm sure they don't plan on it.

8.26.02—Big meeting this weekend for the DRC. They don't know what to do about Zandi and it's driving them nuts. They think it's only going to get worse. I hope so.

9.3.02—Kodama wants to bet on surface games now? Who would have thought, but I'll take his money.

On a more adventurous note, Nick got us into Rebek today. Amazing. I'd love to spend some time there but we had to hurry. He tells me there is a new Age as well with creatures. I'd love to get there but I doubt it will happen. The DRC is sick to their stomach with this Zandi stuff. I'm on his side but I hope this just doesn't make things worse.

9.07.02—Zandi is getting them on his side. I wish I could describe Kodama. Wow. I love it. I did see his sign on the surface. No one ever seemed to notice it though. I guess he's making them. Ha.

9.14.02—Marie has lost it. A t-shirt? I agree with Kodama on that one.

10.14.02—Kodama is taking money from me and it's driving me crazy. If I wasn't watching his veins burst in those meetings, I'd be much more angry. It's worth it though.

11.14.02—Well, Zandi is unstoppable now. He's going to bring people down and they can't stop him. It is funny but it's also more work. I want this to work for everyone so I'm helping out more where I can. Still hoping for leverage on that structure I've been wanting for a few years now anyway.

11.18.02—This Zandi stuff is great. I do think the DRC is going to be ready for them but still . . . more power to him. Amazingly, no one has officially talked to me yet from the DRC.

12.01.02—Looks like URU is it now. Thanks to Zandi, again.

12.24.02—Christmas Eve in Teledahn. If I imagine hard enough, the spores look like
          a Northeast Christmas. Not really. I think I'm heading back for the
          playoffs and New Year.

1.05.03—No playoffs but still a good New Year. This should be a fun year for D'ni.
          Also brought down some more fish tank pieces this trip. I think it's about
          ready. If I get a chance to work on it.

1.07.03—Should be interesting to watch Zandi and the DRC as well. I'll be anxious
          to see who gets the power here.

2.01.03—Looks like they are trying to get the upper hand. Explain the Zandi story
          and be up front about it. Watson had to convince some of his members of
          that one, believe me. But probably smart.

3.15.03—Ages are being approved, visitors are coming down. I'm losing time to write
          journals.

4.2.03—Closing, opening. I don't understand the idea but the DRC is definitely
          trying to get ready for the new arrivals. Another large group just came
          down and it seems as though things are going fairly smooth.

5.4.03—I've heard them talking recently about a house out on the Island. They are
          beginning initial restoration but I've got to find a way on that. Nick says
          the place is amazing. He's read some histories and the stories go on and on
          and way back. I'm going to talk to Watson now.

5.20.03—There are rumors of a D'ni survivor going around here. The DRC is keeping
          it low-key but it seems pretty reliable. Obviously, I'll be the last to hear
          but I've got to find a way to meet him as soon as possible.

6.25.03—Funny. Seems like a lot less people are in the city nowadays. DRC is talking
          quite a bit about visitors' access to Ages that they have not approved. They
          are a little irritated to say the least, and trying to figure out a way they
          can control it. I don't think they can. Interesting.

          Finally got the gun up and working. Laxman is getting better every day.
          The guy is a genius. Watson stopped by as well to see it working although
          he seemed more concerned with me cleaning up the scrap than the gun
          itself. Typical DRC.

7.9.03—Ironic. After all the trouble getting that gun together, I find a whole supply
          of them out on an island. Of course, the guns are just the beginning of
          this place. Some of the reason the DRC wanted me away from there is
          starting to make sense. Who would have thought?

7.18.03—Out of the blue, Sonya Michaels has contacted me. Old friend from the surface working for some paper up in Maine. Says she is coming down for a long period. Wants to write.

On a more typical note, Watson came by a few days ago asking me to name some of the wildlife here. They aren't finding the names the D'ni used for of a lot of the animals. He added that my names need to sound D'ni though. I don't think he really appreciated Shroomie and Flappers. Anyway, I named the birds here Buggaros. I think some part of that is D'ni for big—that's what Nick said at least. Big bug. Wonder how they'll like that?

Found during Gahreesen Journey

Journal: "The KI"

Base Functions—D'ni #3 on the back side of all of these devices . . . 3 functions? There's certainly more than that. 3 core functions? In any case, it's a convenient name: KI.

This journal was discovered in one of the Control Rooms of the Training Facility.

1. Nexus Interface—the Nexus seems to be just an interpreter for KI data. KIs allow users to provide or decline Book access to other KIs. I think we can make this work for neighborhoods as well. Age names defined in the KI appear in the Nexus. Or should. . . .

2. Interpersonal Communication—Obviously the most important function: voice or text communication to other KI users. Inter- or Intra-Age—doesn't seem to matter.

3. Image Capture, Storage & Transfer—A single button-press captures an image and stores it within an appropriate Age directory. Images can be sent to other KIs as well as uploaded to some imagers (depending on versions). Seems main servers coordinated this functionality—might be tough to revive.

4. Journal Entry, Storage & Transfer—fairly simple. Write notes and store them. Again server handles transfer journals ... KI-to-KI or KI-to-imager.

5. Markers—the ability to drop and collect markers at the operator's present location in an Age. Layers of functionality here—requires more research. Perhaps this feature could be tapped to help with the GZ problem ... interesting.

6. Doors—In this Age, the KI (even at its most base level) opened Level 1 doors. Level 2 and 3 doors require higher versions.

There is much more variety to these devices than we first suspected. The "dispenser" is capable of handing out at least five versions and possibly more. Feature set varies widely. There must have been a system to control and track these devices ... where?

Imager built into the unit is surprisingly compact and efficient. Uses this same blasted "lattice" compression system for lack of a better word ... have to crack that. Powerful projection for something that fits on the top of a hand.

MARKERS
Purpose: Perhaps a training tool for Maintainers. Markers could be set up and recruits and/or lower ranks run through the "course."

INTERFACE: KI's INTERACT WITH MARKERS IN 3 WAYS.

— "Team Capture"—once all the markers are placed, there are two teams that can collect markers. The KI registers the marker to the respective team. Markers can vanish after a time limit or after all have been registered. Markers must be in same Age. Test: Can markers be reset?

— "Hold"—again two teams. Markers only vanish after a pre-set time limit has expired. Markers do not disappear upon being activated although server keeps track of what team is "holding" it. Server summarizes team holding most markers at the end of the time limit. Markers must be in same Age.

— "Single Capture"—only one individual KI can register markers. Markers also carry text. Entire marker set can be sent via KI to another KI anywhere in the system. Markers can be placed in any Age.

Markers themselves seem identical to those produced by the Great Zero. In fact, I'm positive the same technology is being used, if not the Great Zero itself. It's possible the KIs are communicating with the Zero itself and writing these marks anywhere they are registered. Problems with that theory ... Maintainer markers, etc. ...

KI REGISTRATION
KI tracks of other KIs on 3 levels:

—Intra-Age: Any other KI within the Age is logged and displayed.

—KI-to-KI: Any individual KI can be registered for specific tracking. As a result, no matter where that KI is, journals, photos, etc. can be sent and communication can occur. Perhaps this was used for temporary or semi-permanent team missions. For our purposes—a 'friends list?'

—Groups: The KI also recognizes groups, somehow related to the Nexus. Seems possible, if properly configured, to support Neighborhood lists with this function.

Journal: Gahreesen

NOTE
This journal was discovered in one of the Control Rooms of the Training Facility. On the cover was a note from Douglas Sharper that read: "Simpson, don't mention anything about the upper area of the fortress in your Gahreesen report. I don't want people wandering all over Teledahn looking for that weird Link stone."

ANALYSIS
Author: Simpson (transcribed from voice recorder)

Age: Gahreesen

Date: 11/12/2001—6/4/02 Multiple trips

Okay, one thing seems immediately obvious: This place was built for security. No one could write a link anywhere in this place, or the next. It was obviously a Maintainer facility of some kind and it doesn't seem that it was for general Guild Members. By that, I mean it was limited to at least the higher-ranking members.

As to how they got the first link written here, I don't know. Probably while it was under construction. It does seem pretty obvious that it's not going to happen again, unless something major happens to this place.

I should say that Kodama has some theories about the Age that have held up so far. May have been a "special forces" of a sort for the Maintainers. Started later, mid-8000s. Became somewhat of a research and development arm for the Maintainers Guild. I don't know, worth mentioning though. There are quite a few mentions of such groups in other docs Kodama has found, or at least seen.

ENTRANCE

To begin with, I'd wager that no one other than a high-ranking government official or similar ever even made it to this room. That's just my guess but it seems pretty sound. I don't think any school buddies or girlfriends dropped by to see their Maintainer friend. The Linking Book we found was deep within the Maintainer Guild. I'm sure it was well guarded in its day.

You can see right off the bat the entrance was extremely secure. Thick walls, one door, a high window (sniper, maybe). If you manage to get in with a bomb or something, it's not going to do any noticeable damage.

I love the Maintainer symbol on the floor and everywhere else you look. As though I might forget and wonder where I am.

WAITING ROOM

So, visitors are escorted into this little waiting room. There's a window on one side, looks almost like a ticket window. Maybe turn in weapons or goods that aren't allowed. Maybe Books. I'm sure they didn't want Books in here.

Yeah, looks like mainly for Books. There is another ticket window on the other side, although this one looks different. I'm pretty sure those are beetle cages on the other side. Beetles that sought out ink. Somebody was just telling me there are all kinds of references to them in other docs. You didn't make it past this room with a Book.

As well, the doors never open at the same time. So, even if somehow you make it out of the entrance room, you're still not going to make it past these mammoth doors out of the waiting area.

HALLS

Looks like the hall ran along the entire circumference of the building. There are plenty of rooms; I'll just try to hit them one at a time. First is an elevator though. However, looks like it's only down. Wonder if it was always that way? More security I guess. Once you've made it into the halls, there is still nowhere to go, at least if they didn't want you going anywhere.

LOCKERS

I would think that any Books that were brought to the Age were kept in the lockers. I'd imagine that some of the workers here or frequent visitors also kept some equipment, but I could be wrong on that. Looks like they kept some Maintainer gear as well; markers, helmets, etc. Seems a little out of place, honestly.

KIs

OK, things are becoming a little more clear now. Just had a long chat with Laxman and researched some different docs over in the city that Nick had. Looks like the current condition I'm seeing was not the original condition.

The KI was a major development not just for the Guild, but also apparently for all citizens. Turns out they were just starting to hand out the KIs to the public around the time of the fall. Nice timing.

So it looks like they had done some renovations in order to facilitate the mass amounts of visitors that would be coming in order to retrieve KIs. Turns out my little girlfriend analogy was pretty much completely wrong. Girlfriends and more were going to start coming here, at least to the open sections. Kodama corrected me. We've actually found multiple Books in neighborhoods, as well as the guarded Maintainer Book I mentioned earlier. Whoops.

So, visitors come in, walk through the doors, beetles check for Books, and they walk down the hall into the KI room. Get a KI and link out. Guards were probably at the up elevator, which is just behind this room. If they did happen to bring any illegal items, they get them back from the other side of the locker room and off they go back home with their new shiny KI.

Makes more sense as to why the Maintainer paraphernalia was in the locker rooms too. Probably a little display type thing for all the visitors. Impress them.

Warehouse

Quite a bit of goodies in here, all of which I'm sure most visitors never saw. Pretty bad cave-in from the floor above, although Engberg says structurally the place seems alright. He's doing more detailed inspections soon.

Looks like most of these crates are filled with KI maintenance-type equipment as well as a variety of spare parts, etc. . . . I don't know. Laxman will have to give this place a good inspection. I'm sure he'll love going through it all. Beyond me, I know that.

Beetle Cages

Convenient cave-in. Not sure how one is supposed to get in the beetle cages without it. No idea how they did it. Link, maybe. Regardless, pretty positive the cages were for beetles. Symbols on the front and quite a bit of remnants in some of the dirtier cages. We'll have to clean those up. Wonder when they all died.

Speaking of access, another question. How'd they get to the second floor? Elevators skip the middle floor. More security, I suppose.

Second Floor

Destruction was a little more substantial than I thought. Looks like it tore out a section of the outer wall even. I'm going to get out of here until Engberg can come back again.

Been a few days, but I'm back. I'm no expert so I guess I have to trust Engberg. But. . . . He says this whole thing is one of the most solid, heavy pieces of construction he's ever seen. It's safe, he assures me. If I die here, and someone retrieves this recording, please sue him for me.

Second floor looks similar to the first; outer hall and a number of rooms. Have to remember that very few people probably ever walked these halls. There is no access via elevators, stairs, anything to get here. I assume it had to be done via a Linking Book, which is probably somewhere in the city. I suppose there could be a way to stop those elevators on the middle floor but I doubt it. Regardless, this floor was extremely secure; Book access only I'm guessing.

Guard Lounge

Next to the observation room—at least that's what I assume it was—is what looks like a guard lounge. Looks like they stayed here for long amounts of time. There are beds in here, as well as couches. I assume these guys manned the window/observation post while visitors were coming in.

GUARD LOCKERS

More lockers, similar to the set downstairs, although these are manned with some heavy equipment. I'm sure Watson will want to see this stuff and keep it locked up well. In fact, I'm not even going to go into detail about it here. Laxman can write all about this stuff in a later report. I will say I didn't know the D'ni had these kinds of technology.

GEAR ROOM

Now I see why this floor was so secure. Looks like the whole power structure for this building is here. Amazing construction. The entire building looks to have been powered by some underground water source that caused it to turn. They implemented a gear that would grab on to teeth in the ground outside, and provide them a power source as well. Talk about killing two giant birds with one stone. Pretty amazing.

Power looks somewhat complicated. Seems as though there were at least occasions that power was turned off, as there are obviously controls to do that, and then start it again. I'm heading to the top.

TOP

Wow. I thought this building was big. The main portion is absolutely giant. And rotating too, of course. I'm overcome with the amount of work put in to this place just for security. It's everywhere. Almost comical picturing government officials walking the same paths I am. Amazing.

To get to the other side, looks like one had to walk across the bridge to the rock pinnacle. The first place since we've arrived that we're able to save a link. And it's not big. And there's a massive structure facing you if you did. Pretty funny to try and picture an army invading. All of them bunched up on this stone waiting for these bridges to rotate—What the? My gosh....

The creatures. These things are something out of a horror movie. I've been up here a little while and I don't see them often but when I do, they are scaring me to death. I'm beginning to understand the fences and structures a little better. Perhaps some of them were designed to keep creatures out more than keep visitors in. Don't hang out in these woods, unless you have a big gun.

Another bridge, to reach the main portion of this place. More security. I will say that the platform between the bridges seems to have eroded. At one time, crossing the bridges was probably a security feature to ensure manageable groups would approach the larger building, one at a time—but I would wager it was still a lot easier than it is now. The erosion to the platform between the bridges has made it a little rougher. I suppose the Maintainers would like it even more in its current condition.

MUD ROOMS

I'm not sure what to call these things, but they remind me of Mud Rooms so I'll call them that. Not much here. Looks like each bridge has a Mud Room attached to it, with another group of doors, etc. . . . There doesn't seem to be any kind of decompression or decontamination that went on here. Really they seem to be nothing more than another spot for another set of doors. Another secure location.

TRAINING CENTER

I was going to go through each of the rooms here, but after making a quick overview, I think I'll just start with the entire thing.

There are three types of rooms in the building, two of each kind. There is a Control Room, one purple and one yellow, a Display Room, one purple and one yellow, and then a Conference Room. Though these aren't colored, I assume there is one for each "team."

The entire building seems to be centered on the massive wall in the middle. The Control Rooms control the wall, the Display Rooms display the uniforms that were worn in the wall (I presume) and the Conference Rooms allow the government visitors and high-ranking officials to confer about those training on the wall. See.

So Control Rooms first.

CONTROL ROOMS

I'm not going to go into controls for the wall in this doc. I'll let Laxman do that at some other time. Regardless, the panel here obviously controls the wall. The wall was used for training as well as testing of various suits. I believe the central room can get pretty hot, cold, smoky, or anything else I can imagine, pretty quick. It was a competition—whoever could get to the top the quickest. Teams would set up the obstacles and members would race.

There is a side tunnel that provides access to the Display Rooms from the Control Room.

DISPLAY ROOMS

Not sure that these were originally Display Rooms—or maybe they were. Either way, there are quite a few old Maintainer suits in here. There is also the latest Maintainer suit (or skin) here. I guess I should say the machine to put on the latest Maintainer suit is in here.

Now that we've had some time to look at this, it's incredible. We're talking about a suit that was skin tight, and had linking abilities, etc. built in. Very hi-tech as far as Maintainer suits go. Very impressive. A Maintainer would fall down the chute and while "traveling" to the interior room/the wall, the suit would be placed on him. I'm begging to try this thing but DRC is insistent no one does. Laxman already has someone on it, trying to figure out more. I'm first when they do.

I think these rooms could basically be described as team locker rooms.

CONFERENCE ROOMS

Well I guess these rooms were where the bigwigs sat down and talked about their Maintainers. Obviously they are set-up to watch the wall, and there are displays that show the patterns being built and "played" on the wall. We'll never know but I can see the Guild Masters in here watching their men compete, preparing to send them out to some radioactive fireball Age to see if their new suits can stand the elements.

UPPER PORTIONS

I'm not going up now but we do know the upper portions were used as prison cells. Typical D'ni technology—they had a single Linking Book that went to all the cells. Since the building was always rotating, a very complicated linking apparatus and timing mechanism was associated with the Book. The timing of the link would determine which cell the person linked into. Apparently, it was very tight.

Speaking of linking. This entire building is rotating as well. It seems that most visitors came from the path from the well, although there were also Books directly to this building. There had to be. It seems that many of them also used the timing mechanism to link into specific rooms. Looks like another new feature designed and built by these guys. One of many I'm sure.

I'm just wondering where the main research labs were? Or better yet, where did everyone sleep or eat?

Found during Eder Gira and Eder Kemo Journey

Letter: From Dr. Watson to Matthew

Matthew,

The last batch of papers you sent were very interesting. Good work. Since you did such a good job, I've got another list I'd like you to divvy up to the team. How you do it is up to you.

I'd like some more information on family life: ceremonies, etc. . . . Anything related to birth, marriage, cultural events. I know we have quite a bit of source material for this so anything you get would be helpful. I think we've gathered quite a bit on science and technology and not enough on the personal lives of these people.

We have quite a bit of Guild information but gathering that all up into one tidy area would be nice.

The Fall is still an obvious area where we are lacking. I'm not sure I can help you with research material but given the latest information we are getting, at some time, we are going to have to dig into this. I recommend assigning someone the sole task of The Fall.

Continue on with the Kings. A short synopsis of all the kings would be helpful following the form you started with the last batch.

We still have religious writings we need to translate. These are going to be the most difficult but I think they can give us large amounts of helpful information.

We have a stack of journals from various D'ni residences, etc. . . . not to mention Ages.

Again, I think that will be more than enough for now. Again, thank your team and tell them they are doing great work.

—Dr. Watson

This letter was discovered in the DRC field office on a D'ni rooftop, which was reached via a Linking Stone in Lower Gira.

Note: From Nick

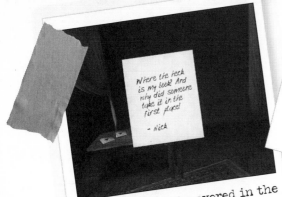

This note was discovered in the DRC field office on a D'ni rooftop, which was reached via a Linking Stone in Lower Gira.

Where the heck is my book? And why did someone take it in the first place!

—Nick

This note was discovered on top of the remnants of a Journey Cloth in the DRC field office on a D'ni rooftop, which was reached via a Linking Stone in Lower Gira.

Note: From Nick

Check this out. I know the DRC doesn't want us to touch these, but I bet Watson would like to know how these register with the doors too. It makes no sense.

And don't lose it. I could barely get it off the wall, and when I did, it was pretty scary. Maybe the weirdest thing is that when I went back later, the cloth I got this piece from was intact again.

—Nick

Journal: Class Structure

Seems as though my first inclination
toward class structure was incorrect.
Though early on there was little in the
way of a class society, such a high ideal
faded quickly. By 9400 DE there were
seven very distinct classes.

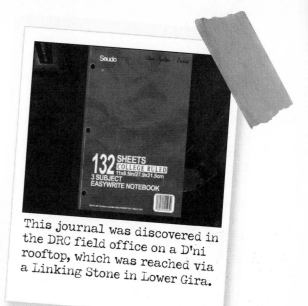

This journal was discovered in
the DRC field office on a D'ni
rooftop, which was reached via
a Linking Stone in Lower Gira.

—Elite: The Lords and the Grand Masters
of the Major Guilds. It was possible for
private citizens to be accepted but, if
so, abundant monetary resources were
needed. It was only the elite who
owned private libraries of Books and
the private Islands.

—Guild Members: Yes it was possible for
the lower classes to attend but it seems by the end
the schools were far too expensive and prestigious to allow for such. As a result, the
graduates became a class among themselves. And a very high one at that.

—Upper Class: The lowers of the three higher classes. Such citizens had succeeded in
private enterprise and most likely provided the elite with their banks, pubs, etc. . . .
No Major Guild education for the most part, but enough money to buy their way into
the upper classes.

—Middle Class: Mostly shop-owners and the like. Able to afford some luxuries of D'ni
but still considered far from the Elite. Rare, but possible, for them to own Books as
well as Private Ages. Seemed to make up most of the Minor Guild enrollment.

—High Poor: The higher class of poor seemed to be made mostly of industrial workers,
many of whom spent their time on foreign Ages (before it was outlawed of course). It
seems that this class, along with the lower two, did not own Books.

—Low Poor: I can't seem to find a better name for them. However, seems clear that there
were two classes of poor. These low poor were relegated to their own districts and
rarely seen even with the middle class and never with the upper classes. Possibly
used as servants, although that was generally looked down upon.

—Sub-Low?: Reference to "the Least" (an undefined sub-class?) are found on rare
occasions. Not enough data to elucidate.

Quite a few obvious attempts to reach out and unify the classes, although I'm not sure
it did much good. Common Libraries, Major Guild scholarships, renovation of poorer
districts, all seemed more political than life changing. Not surprising I suppose.

Journal: Pregnancy

Now this is surprising. I can't say for sure but it seems fairly clear that D'ni women were only fertile for one D'ni "day" every two D'ni "months." In surface terms, that's roughly only thirty hours every seventy-two days.

If true, it explains quite a few things. First, why there were so few children for a people who lived three hundred years and secondly the reason behind the rather large celebrations of pregnancy.

This journal was discovered in the DRC field office on a D'ni rooftop, which was reached via a Linking Stone in Lower Gira.

As far as I can tell, these celebrations were usually limited to family members although they were rather large. There was quite a bit of prayer to Yahvo, as well as blessings from the family members. These "blessings" usually included vows to care for the pregnant woman and child through the coming months.

As I have mentioned in other areas, pregnant women were believed to be much more insightful and as a result, part of the pregnancy experience (although not part of the official ceremony) was using that insight to gain revelation from Yahvo. Though there was quite a bit of religious meditation expected of women during this time, I won't go into it here. However, this meditation was expected to primarily guide the women to her child's future, and its purpose and was taken rather seriously.

While pregnancy within marriage was cause for great celebration, the same cannot be said of pregnancy outside of marriage. As far as I can tell, any woman who became pregnant was expected to immediately marry and any child conceived out of wedlock was unable to join a Guild for its entire life. As well, no revelation was expected from such a mother. Such a curse was just as horrible for a lower-class woman, as her child would have no chance of ever attending the Guilds of the upper class and thus gaining status.

As far as I can see, gestation was a full year. Ten D'ni months—290 D'ni days—equivalent to one Earth year. I have found no records of multiple births.

Journal: Maturity

Similar to a variety of other cultures, the D'ni celebrated a child's entrance into reason and maturity. The D'ni believed that true maturity, or the Age of Reason as they called it, was achieved at the age of twenty-five. Before that, the D'ni believed that children's minds and hearts were not properly formed. Up until that time they even went so far as to say it was impossible for a child to truly make a correct decision as they were too easily controlled by other motives. That did not mean that what they did was not right or wrong but the D'ni believed that Yahvo did not hold them accountable for those decisions. Up to that point, it was apparently up to the parents to judge and protect and thus another reason society encouraged couples to only have one child at a time under twenty-five.

This journal was discovered in the DRC field office on a D'ni rooftop, which was reached via a Linking Stone in Lower Gira.

In the "ceremony of readiness," the D'ni celebrated a child's entrance into reason and maturity.

At the ceremony, the child was presented with a bracelet of knowledge (also translated "maturity"). I have to admit the translation is somewhat poor and makes it sound like a magical or superstitious item—a translation that does not fit the way they talk about it. In fact, it was a very serious item.

The D'ni viewed the bracelet as a sign of accountability. The individual, once given the bracelet, was expected to be responsible for his/her actions as he/she had true knowledge of good and evil and the wisdom to make the right choices between both. Associated with the bracelet were certain rights, as well as expectations to behave in a more correct manner.

From a religious standpoint, the "ceremony of readiness" signaled accountability to Yahvo, as well as fellow D'ni citizens. No longer were parents judged for the actions of their children on a religious level, and no longer was lack of knowledge an excuse to Yahvo. The Maker, they believed, now expected much more from them.

Though the Age of Reason was twenty-five, the D'ni did not consider true wisdom to come until much later. With not nearly the fanfare that the Age of Reason brought, at 125 years of age there was another celebration for reaching the Age of Wisdom. Perhaps most importantly, regarding that status, the D'ni were then allowed to reach the highest ranks of teachers or leaders (Grand Masters or Lords).

The same rules applied to women, and no woman under the age of 125 was technically allowed to advise, especially to the Kings. As well, it appears that a woman's fertility ended around age 125.

During the time of the Kings, advisors were required for those Kings who were under the age of 125, as the King himself had not achieved the Age of Wisdom. The Great King Ahlsendar was the only King who did not have an official advisor even though he was under the Age of Wisdom for the majority of his reign.

Journal: Marriage

Much more than modern cultures, within D'ni culture all citizens were expected to marry. In fact, it was even believed that marriage was an important part of a relationship with Yahvo as it taught and revealed the necessary requirements for such a relationship. Both marriage relationships and the relationship with Yahvo were described by the same D'ni word, taygahn. Literally translated, the word means "to love with the mind," and implied a deep understanding, respect, and most importantly, unselfish love for one another.

This journal was discovered in the DRC field office on a D'ni rooftop, which was reached via a Linking Stone in Lower Gira.

Obviously the religious influence on most of D'ni culture was very strong and, as a result, marriage was not something taken lightly. It was considered a lifetime commitment and, for a D'ni who could live to be 300 years old, it obviously was not a decision the D'ni felt should be rushed into and it seems as though it rarely was.

Some records point to rare arranged marriages, although for the most part it seems that the decision was up to individuals. Marriage was not permitted before the age of 25 and marriage between blood relatives was strictly forbidden. Though allowed, marriage between the classes was looked down upon. Marriage to other worlders was practically unheard of. I've found certain writings from the 9000s going so far as to call the mixing of D'ni blood with outside cultures a travesty, while others wrote such a child (who marries an outsider) was better off dead. Even so, there are reports in other documents of Kings even marrying outsiders. I'm a little confused. . . .

The marriage ceremony itself was not a single-day event, but one that took over five days. Attendance to those sections of the ceremony to which one was invited was extremely important and it was considered a disgrace to be invited and not attend.

The event usually began with a small ceremony held on the evening before the First Day of the marriage ceremony. The ceremony always took place at the home of the groom (or his parents) and was meant to confirm both the bride and groom's decision to be united to one another in front of their immediate family.

The groom presented his bride-to-be with a gift representing the confirmation of his choice. The acceptance of the gift by the bride-to-be was acknowledgment of her decision. Immediately after her acceptance of the gift, the bride-to-be was escorted away with her family and not to be seen by her groom until the Joining Ceremony that would take place on the Fifth Day.

The First Day was meant for the bride and groom to spend time with their families. As they were starting their own family, their old family would no longer be the highest priority. Thus, the day was set aside to spend time with that original family. Traditionally, the day ended with a large meal as well as speeches and blessings from the parents to the child.

The Second Day was set aside for the bride and groom to spend with friends, both married and unmarried. Traditionally, one of the friends would host a large dinner at the end of the day.

The Third Day was reserved for spending time with the soon-to-be in-laws. It was on that day that the bride and groom received blessings from their in-laws as well as other members of the family. Again, there was a traditional larger meal at the end of the day marked by speeches from the eventual in-laws and other soon-to-be family members.

The Fourth Day was meant for the couple to spend time alone with Yahvo, individually. Though many apparently viewed the day as a formality, others viewed it as the most significant of all the days. The day was often filled with prayer asking for Yahvo's blessings upon the event as well as a time to understand Yahvo's desires for their new lives together. It was also considered a time to purify themselves before Yahvo. Some chose to spend time with the priests or prophets, while others read the Holy Books and talked to Yahvo himself.

The Fifth Day was the Day of Joining. The early portion of the day was set aside for physical preparation, while the later part of the day was set aside for the Joining Ceremony itself.

For those who did not have access to Private Ages, the ceremony usually took place on "Marriage Ages." For the upper classes, the ceremony took place in Family Ages. All family was expected to attend, as were fellow Guild members.

All of those in attendance were divided into two sides. One side represented the groom while the other represented the bride. Between the two sides, in the center, was a long aisle and a triangular podium. The bride and groom would each approach their side of the podium by walking through their respective family and friends. It was after all, those family and friends who had made the bride and groom what they were, and the D'ni believed it was those family and friends who should "present" the bride or groom to their spouse. The priest usually stood on the third side of the podium.

As with most important events, and especially marriage, the bride and groom wore the bracelets they had been given at birth as well as maturity. After the bride and groom arrived to the platform, the father of the bride would remove the bride's bracelets and give them to the groom. The D'ni believed the giving of the bracelets represented the giving of the bride's purity and adulthood to the groom. A short speech often followed the event. The father of the groom would follow the father of the bride with the identical procedure, giving his son to the bride.

The giving of the children was followed by an expression of both parents of their blessings upon those being joined, as well as all of those present. Symbolically, the bride and groom then switched sides to represent an acceptance of all the bride's family and friends of the groom and visa versa. Both the bride and groom then handed all four bracelets to the priest.

While the priest led the couple through their commitments to one another and Yahvo, the bride and groom placed their hands upon the podium. During the commitments, the couple made promises to one another followed by promised to Yahvo. All were recited aloud.

The priest usually reminded the couple that marriage was a reminder of taygahn (to know with the mind) and that their love should always be a representation of their love for Yahvo.

Following the commitments, the priest would place two new, and larger, bracelets upon the bride and groom. The groom's was placed upon the left wrist and the bride the right wrist. The new bracelets were meant to represent both the purity and maturity bracelets their spouse had previously worn. The D'ni emphasized that the spouse was now your responsibility to keep pure and knowledgeable of good and evil. The bracelets were meant to be a constant reminder of that responsibility, as well as the commitment to maintain the best for that spouse.

After the new bracelets were placed upon the wrists, the hands of the bride and groom were wrapped together with a tight cord, covering the wrist and hands completely. Upon completion, the priest placed a ring upon the pinky of each "free" hand. The rings were symbolic reminders of the entire ceremony and placed upon the fifth finger to represent the joining that took place on the fifth day.

The priest would then usually remove him/herself from the podium so that the couple could take his/her place. Together, the couple then walked down the aisle between the two "parties" and toward the far end of the aisle where a glass of wine waited for them. Before drinking, the couple knelt and prayed together to Yahvo.

After the prayer, they each drank from the cup and the two sides of the hall merged into one group, often with great celebration. They were now considered joined and the celebration could begin.

Families usually fed all in attendance and there was typically dancing and music. The couple was expected to keep their hands united throughout the night as a reminder that they were now joined, both in the eyes of man and Yahvo. The binding of the hands was apparently meant to be somewhat troublesome, symbolizing that there would be difficult times to their relationship but that those times did not affect the fact they were now joined.

Following the celebrations, tradition was for the couple to embrace and the priest to hold a Linking Book to their skin so that they would both link to "vacation" or "honeymoon" type Ages. Though these vacations were usually short, it was not unusual for the man to not work for up to a year in order to build the new marriage.

I should also note that the cord used to join the couple's hands together was also viewed as a sacred item. It seems as though various couples used the cords in a variety of different ways; some using them for necklaces and others hanging them in their house.

Journal: King Ri'neref

Ri'neref was born in 207 BE (Before Earth) on Garternay. He was accepted into the Guild of Writers at the age of five (a standard age) and, as the years passed, quickly became one of the finest Writers that the Ronay had ever seen. Certain records go as far as stating that Ri'neref was "unsurpassed in skill" by any other Writer of the day.

By the time he was 90, Ri'neref had achieved the rank of Guild Master and was well on his way to become the Grand Master. However, due to personal convictions, he never achieved that rank.

This journal was discovered in the DRC field office on a D'ni rooftop, which was reached via a Linking Stone in Lower Gira.

Ri'neref had long been a challenger of the views of the Guild of Writers, as well as the King himself. Ri'neref was apparently very concerned with the society's views pertaining to the purpose of writing and the challenge of acting responsibly with the " . . . great gift given to us by Yahvo."[2]

Around 73 BE, Ri'neref was asked by the Grand Master to write a Descriptive Book to a questionable Age . . . at least in the eyes of Ri'neref. He perceived the Age being used to house an uncivilized race that could be used for the purposes of the Ronay. Thus, Ri'neref refused to carry out the command from his Grand Master and, after much debating, was apparently dismissed from the Guild of Writers. Some records do point to Ri'neref willfully excusing himself from the Guild, although regardless of how he left, much of the society found the "dismissal" unfair and some even went so far as to call it "detrimental to society."[3]

Around 59 BE, the fact that Garternay would not be able to serve the Ronay as a home for much longer[4] was confirmed and the information made public. Ri'neref had long known of the state of Garternay and from the time of his dismissal had apparently been working on an Age that he felt would be a good place to live for those who wished to follow him.

According to various journals, Ri'neref managed to attract a few thousand Ronay and convince them to follow him in the ways that he felt important and to the Age that he had written. The King allowed Ri'neref to split away from the Ronay, along with a few other smaller groups, while the majority of Ronay left Garternay to a new home world called Terahnee. Ri'neref took his group to Earth, where he established the D'ni (meaning "New Beginning").

Ri'neref was a strong leader, immediately establishing himself as King and reigning for 120 years until his death. Obviously, those who followed Ri'neref to D'ni already respected him enough to separate themselves from their family and friends, and thus, records point to very few debates or disagreements within the society under the reign of Ri'neref.

As had always been the case with the Ronay, a group of surveyors was sent to D'ni, before the group officially moved there, to establish the Great Zero[5] and the line emanating from it. A monument was built on the Great Zero in the year 0 DE.

Unlike previous occasions, Ri'neref established the line of the Great Zero as set apart for holy buildings. Without authorization by the reigning King, construction was forbidden.

Though it's never stated directly, records strongly imply that it was Ri'neref who chose where the city would be established. He seemed to base his decision on two factors (which probably made the decision an easy one). First was the line of the Great Zero. It seemed an obvious spot to base the city, with the most important religious structures being directly on the line and the rest of the city surrounding its center. The second factor was a group of waterfalls that flowed from the ceiling of the cavern to an area adjacent to the line of the Great Zero. The fresh flowing water was perfect for drinking.

A new Writer's Guild (with fairly different rules than the one that had existed on Garternay) was constructed almost immediately (8 DE) under the direction of Ri'neref. By the year 100 DE Ri'neref had directed the re-creation of the 18 Major Guilds.[6] The Guilds were dedicated to Yahvo on "The Day of the Circle," a celebration not only of the completion of the Major Guilds, but a celebration of New Guilds, which Ri'neref believed were "healthier" than those that existed in Garternay.

"Guilds that have been established to please Yahvo and not themselves. . . . " Ri'neref said.[7] Certain records point to the Guilds on Garternay becoming extremely competitive with one another and focusing more upon having the best facility than carrying out their duty to Yahvo and the people. In an effort to curb that kind of competition, Ri'neref implemented a list of restrictions upon Guild construction. The restrictions included guidelines pertaining to placement (facing the Great Zero), size, shape, and minor visual guidelines.

Though one of Ri'neref's top priorities was construction of a Temple, there were disagreements as to specifics, causing numerous delays in the finalization of construction plans. Eventually, construction was started in 48 DE and the Temple was completed in 63 DE. Known as the Regeltovokum, the Temple to Yahvo was meant as a place of worship as well as a reminder of the prophesied Great King who would come to them soon.[8]

Ri'neref also made it a priority to install massive fans that would supply the cavern with fresh air. Natural openings existed but it was quickly discovered that they did not supply ample circulation for the cavern. As a result, massive shafts and fans were built and installed over a thirty-year period between 84 and 114 DE. It should be noted that numerous records point to a small group of D'ni disappearing upon completion of the fans. It is most often assumed that they remained on the surface of Earth to live.

Throughout his reign, records point to multiple occasions on which Ri'neref refused to build a palace for himself. Instead, he lived in a fairly basic home, similar in fashion to most of his fellow citizens and made it especially clear that until Yahvo had a new home, he could not allow himself one. Although, even after the Temple was completed, Ri'neref refused to build a palace, always focusing more on the religious and government sites. Ri'neref's own philosophy centered on the fact that it was much easier to focus on Yahvo and his wishes when circumstances were difficult and struggles more abundant. It was strongly believed that Ri'neref's refusal to build a palace was an expression of that philosophy.

In 120 DE, Ri'neref died of apparent heart complications. He was 327 years old. Though he had married, he left no children. As a result, he chose one of his apprentices, named Ailesh, to succeed him.

NOTES

1. Taken from the Memoirs of Ailesh.

2. From the Oath of the New Guild of Writers written by Ri'neref.

3. Taken from the journals of Grand Master Najun of the Guild of Legislators.

4. Garternay's sun was dying and would eventually cause a rapid decrease in temperature, making it an uninhabitable Age.

5. The Great Zero itself was usually based on a prominent natural landmark within an Age. From the Great Zero a line was drawn, usually toward magnetic north, to aid in navigation, construction, etc.

6. It should be noted that the 18 Major Guilds of D'ni were not necessarily the same as the 18 that had existed on Ronay. In fact, they were probably much different. Though there is no information that details the Major Guilds of Ronay, we do know that the Guilds were meant to be flexible and serve the people in the needs of their time.

7. Taken from a transcript of Ri'neref's speech on the first Day of the Circle.

8. The prophetical work the Regeltavok of Oorpah, a book Ri'neref believed strongly in, dealt with numerous prophesies of a Great King who would be sent by Yahvo to guide the people.

Journal: King Ailesh

Ailesh took the throne in coronation ceremonies in the year 120 DE at the age of 170. Though it seems Ailesh had never been a member of the Writer's Guild on Garternay, he had spent the first fifty years of his life with Ri'neref (after his own dismissal) working on the Book of D'ni. When the D'ni Writer's Guild was formed in the year 8 DE, Ri'neref made sure Ailesh was placed in charge as the first Grand Master of the Guild.

This journal was discovered in the DRC field office on a D'ni rooftop, which was reached via a Linking Stone in Lower Gira.

As Grand Master, he had worked closely with Ri'neref in the writing of the new Guild of Writer's Oath. The Oath, which was what every member promised to live by, ended up staying in existence (with few minor changes) until 9400 DE.

Records indicate that Ailesh modeled his life very closely to Ri'neref's. He refused to build himself a palace until a Common Library was opened; as he strongly supported a place where all citizens could have access to Books. Though there was some minor disagreement on minor issues the building was eventually finished in 233 DE. Although, like his mentor, Ailesh still refused to build himself a palace.

The reign of Ailesh was extremely similar to that of Ri'neref. There was still great excitement for the new ideals and laws of D'ni, and thus great support for Ailesh, making his reign a very smooth one.

Before his third son was born in 256 DE, records indicate that there was a bit of public apprehension over who the next King would be. Ailesh's two eldest sons were fairly rebellious and neither seemed good candidates for the throne, at least in the public's opinion. However, as Ailesh's third son grew, it became apparent to the public (although records never give specific reasons) that the boy closely followed his father's ideals. Ailesh must have agreed with public opinion as it was his third son who he selected to succeed him.

Ailesh died of natural causes at the age of 350.

Journal: King Shomat

Shomat took the throne in the year 300 DE (D'ni Era) at the age of 44. Up to the point of his coronation, he had been a member of the Guild of Writers. He continued his study of the Art through private mentors for a number of years after his coronation. It was the lack of proper Guild instruction that most D'ni historians attribute the distorted views Shomat later took on.

This journal was discovered in the DRC field office on a D'ni rooftop, which was reached via a Linking Stone in Lower Gira.

It was an up-and-down reign, partly due to a tremendous tension that seemed to exist between himself and his older brothers. Both of the brothers, though they had little respect, did everything in their power to make Shomat's reign tumultuous.

One of the first actions Shomat ordered was construction of a palace. When it was completed in 347 DE, Shomat moved in with his family, although his brothers refused, and maintained their own homes. Such an act was regarded as a tremendous disrespect to a family and only served to widen the gap between Shomat and his brothers.

Furthering tensions not only within Shomat's family but within the culture as well was the lavishness of the palace. Ornate gardens were present inside the physical grounds and "garden" Ages were written as well, linking from within the palace. Rumors abounded that some of these "garden" Ages were even wiped of their inhabitants in order to provide Shomat with relaxation. Whether true or not, Shomat often spoke publicly of the need for Ages to serve D'ni. This was a first for the society and a direct contradiction to what the Guilds taught: the D'ni were to "serve" the Ages.

It seems that eventually the tension became too much. Some say it drove Shomat mad. In 387 DE both his brothers disappeared and were never found again. It was commonly presumed that Shomat wrote a Death Book to which both of his brothers were linked into, although it could never be proven.

Regardless, it was one of the first major challenges for the people of D'ni and they reacted quickly. A prophetess[1] was supplied to Shomat in 400 DE in an attempt to guide him in the ways of Yahvo.[2] For the 155 remaining years of his reign, it seems that most people believed Shomat became a better King. The prophetess became an excellent mentor for Shomat and eventually convinced him to choose the son of one of his close friends as the heir to the throne. His own children were admittedly "out of control." As it turns out, it was the bloodline of that child that led to the birth of the Great King years later.

Shomat died of natural causes at the age of 299.

NOTES

1. Women were generally seen as much better communicators with Yahvo than men. As a result, most prophets were women.

2. The choosing of prophetesses, as guides for the Kings, started with Shomat and became tradition for all the remaining Kings of D'ni. It was usually up to the King as to which prophet or prophetess he would seek for wisdom.

Journal: King Naygen

Naygen took the throne in 2356 DE at the age of 86. Naygen did much to encourage the growth of the Major Guild of Fine Artists, as well as the seeking of the other "truths." The year 2500 DE (1,000 years after the death of the Great King) would mark the peak of what some would call "the religious confusion."[1] There were over 2,000 registered sects and the original beliefs of Ri'neref were known by very few. Naygen was clearly not one of them.

This journal was discovered in the DRC field office on a D'ni rooftop, which was reached via a Linking Stone in Lower Gira.

It is 2397 DE that most officially marked the start of the D'ni Renaissance. In that year, the Eamis Theatre Company hosted the first play written by the playwright Sirreh. The play dealt with the Pento War and the Great King himself and was one which Naygen praised. It ended up being sold out for three straight weeks and marked not only the start of theatre as a popular entertainment source within the culture, but also the beginning of the Pento War subject, which would go on to become one of the most dealt with topics of their history in their Art.

In 2408 DE, the 33-year-old musician Airem began selling out concert halls, marking the beginning of yet another career of one of the great D'ni artists. His music also dealt much with the Great King, many times ridiculing him. Naygen praised his people for being able to express "their true feelings in such wonderful displays of art."[2]

In 2488 DE, the first successful extrusion tests were carried out by the Guild of Miners, and to great applause from the public. Naygen used the occasion to "benefit everyone." He appointed the Guild of Miners as a Major Guild replacing the Guild of Fine Artists. He then split the Guild of Fine Artists up into the Minor Guilds of Sculptors, Artists, Actors, and Musicians. The split was to encourage growth in mining as well as the arts, two major causes of Naygen throughout his reign. His proposal was strongly supported by Sirreh and Airem, as well as other artists, who viewed it as an excellent opportunity for the growth of their respective fields.

In 2500 DE, Naygen proposed the construction of a new Council chamber for the Guilds. Somewhat surprising was that he suggested it should be built over the Tomb of the Great King. The proposal was met with little opposition,[3] and construction began two years later. In 2504 DE, the Tomb of the Great King was barely visible, a tremendous symbol of what D'ni had become.

Later it was discovered that within the Council chamber was a massive vault, protected by "puzzles" of a sort. The tomb had always been known for its patterns, some of which were claimed to have prophetic messages. Naygen apparently became enamored with the patterns and spread them throughout the unseen portions of the chamber as well as the seen. Though the public knew very little of the vault at the time of construction, years later it was found to contain a tremendous amount of royal wealth, something Naygen often publicly encouraged. Of course, most were not able to save the amounts Naygen did, but still the idea of saving one's money for future generations was strongly encouraged by him.

Naygen died in 2533 DE at the age of 263 leaving the throne to his third son. In memorial to Naygen, Sirreh wrote another of the more popular of his plays entitled "Our Great King." It was the first play performed by the Minor Guild of Actors in 2535 DE.

NOTES

1. Taken from the journal of Tevahr in 3075.

2. From a speech by Naygen, christening the Minor Guild of Musicians.

3. Though the official Church registered a complaint, it seemed there was little heart behind it. Apparently, even a prophetess of Naygen supported the proposition.

Journal: King Demath

Demath took the throne in 4692 DE at the age of 154. Though the public was generally not happy with the reign of Ji, it appears as though they were pleased with his choice of Demath to succeed him.[1]

Demath had joined the Guild of Maintainers at the age of five (as most did) and risen to the level of Guild Master by the time he was chosen as King. The selection was a surprise to much of the public, and apparently even to Demath himself. It was not a post he had especially desired to have.

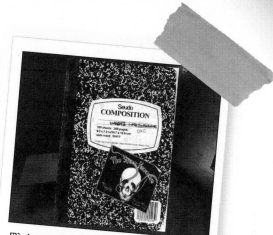

This journal was discovered in the DRC field office on a D'ni rooftop, which was reached via a Linking Stone in Lower Gira.

Almost immediately, Demath ordered a ban on all unnecessary Links (to be enforced by the Maintainers) while the Council carried out emergency meetings, trying to decide their stance on the outsiders.

In these meetings, the Council concluded that relations with the outsiders would continue, but with much stricter restrictions and guidelines. The list was long that Demath signed into law and included the restriction of any outsiders operating D'ni machinery or Linking Books.

Perhaps more importantly, the Council and King sent a clear message to all of the factions who were against outsider involvement with D'ni; their ideas would not be tolerated if they led to any infraction of the rules previously established by Loshemanesh, which were to become strictly enforced. And though it was not stated publicly, the Relyimah (meaning "the Unseen") was apparently ordered to double its membership and find any and all who were carrying out illegal activities with the outsiders.

As well, Demath denounced the words of the Watcher as pure rubbish and nothing more than "a desperately lonely man seeking attention."[2]

In 4721 DE, Demath pushed an amendment that forced the Major Guilds to accept a percentage of students who passed all entrance exams but could not afford the steep prices.[3] It was the first such action in the history of D'ni and one that many seemed to question, especially the Guilds themselves. However, Demath was able to convince them it was a necessity for the society and one to which they "cautiously agreed."[4]

In 4724 DE, records point to over ten separate groups being convicted of the Loshemanesh Laws (as they had come to be called). Most agreed that the Relyimah played a large role in the convictions although there are no official records of their involvement. Regardless, each of the convicted was sentenced to solitary confinement on Prison Ages. The convictions must have carried a powerful impact on the society, as the public still knew very little of the Relyimah (if anything at all), and thus had no idea how so many convictions were occurring. As one writer said, "There were stories of dark shadows and mysterious creatures . . . for those carrying out such activities . . . it was said that the eyes of Demath saw everything while his arms took anyone he wanted."[5] The crime rate, especially pertaining to the Loshemanesh Laws, steadily lowered until 4752, when there were only three recorded convictions.

In 4784 DE, an assassination attempt was carried out against Demath resulting in the death of two members of the Relyimah, who saved Demath's life in the process. The perpetrators were found and two years later, Demath ordered their execution. It was the first execution of its kind and met with little resistance from the public or Council. The two men were apparently linked into a Death Age, permanently ending their lives. Though most agreed with the execution, those who were against outsider involvement to begin with now felt even stronger in their case. Now, they argued, "D'ni is killing itself, for the sake of the outsiders."[6]

In 4826, Demath was rewarded for his efforts pertaining to the acceptance policies of the Major Guilds. The first of the Guild of Stone Masons' "non-paying" members headed the effort to devise early fusion-compounding technology, a building block for the eventual development of Nara. Demath praised the Guild and the numerous opportunities that all citizens of D'ni now had to benefit their society.[7]

In 4843 at the age of 305, Demath passed away leaving the throne to his first-born son.

NOTES

1. Some argued that Ji didn't make the choice of Demath but that Grand Master Imas of the Guild of Maintainers made it. The matter was never officially settled although most contribute the choice to Ji.

2. From Demath's speech, explaining to the people the findings of the Council meetings.

3. By that time, the Major Guilds had become extremely expensive and a large majority of the population, even if qualified to join the Guilds, had no way to afford it.

4. Taken from the private journals of Guild Master Reshan of the Guild of Archivists.

5. From Revealing the Unseen written by Besharen in 5999.

6. Goshen, leader of the cult group Blood of Yahvo, made the comment in a public speech.

7. The comments were made by Demath at the public announcement of the fusion-compounding technology.

Journal: King Me'emen

Me'emen took the throne in 5240 DE at the age of 83.

One of the biggest announcements of Me'emen's reign came rather quickly and was offered by the Guild of Miners and Stone Masons (who had worked together). In 5307 they revealed Nara[1], which had been created in a laboratory weeks earlier. Nara offered tremendous opportunities for mining and construction and ended up having a massive impact on future opportunities for D'ni. Even at the time of its release, there was apparently much excitement about its potential.

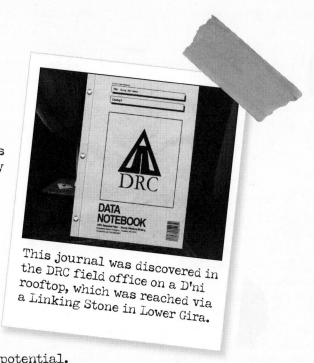

This journal was discovered in the DRC field office on a D'ni rooftop, which was reached via a Linking Stone in Lower Gira.

In 5312 DE, disease broke out in the industrial district of D'ni, most likely originating in the Age of Yasefe.[2] The outbreak caused widespread panic as many predicted another plague similar to what had occurred during the 2100s. Fortunately, the illness was not nearly as lethal as the aforementioned, and the Guild of Healers reacted extraordinarily fast in finding a cure. Regardless, there was again a new push to at least separate the Nehw'eril District[3] far away from the city proper.

Me'emen apparently liked the idea quite a bit and encouraged the Surveyors to begin looking into such an expansion.

In 5359 DE, the D'ni received another great reason to begin major expansion and it came in the form of Stone Tooth. It was the second of the Great Diggers and quite a bit more powerful and technologically advanced than the older Stone Eater. Me'emen immediately ordered the Guild of Miners to begin "clearing" an area (along with Stone Eater) for a new industrial district replacing Nehw'eril. It was not until 5475 DE that actual construction was begun on the new industrial section Uran.

Less than a hundred years after Stone Tooth, in 5473 DE, the Guild of Maintainers announced that the newly discovered Deretheni could be used to create much improved, and much more protective, Maintainer suits. Though such an announcement may not seem especially important, the new suits ended up having a great impact on D'ni culture. Since the Maintainers were able to take bigger risks with the types of Ages they could explore, the Guild of Writers were allowed to be a bit more liberal in their writing, and a new breed of Age was begun.[4]

During Me'emen's reign "Words" became a common topic of discussion and attention was again given to the older temples. Evidence points to numerous remodels and renovations of many of the secular temples that had been built years earlier on the "new" line of the Great Zero.

It seems that Me'emen himself paid little attention to the religious pulse of his people being much more interested in technological advancements and city expansion to care.

Once Me'emen felt that Stone Eater and Stone Tooth were no longer needed, he recommended using them to build an underground tunnel connecting The Island to the city proper, and minimizing the need for boat travel. His proposition was not embraced by any means, especially by the upper classes who were living on The Island. Apparently there were a number of protests, for fear of the affect the tunnel could have on The Island. The proposal was also rejected by most of the Guilds, causing Me'emen to not force it.

In 5500 DE, the first imports from other Ages were linked to the new Uran District, much farther from the city. Uran was said to be "a tremendous improvement over the older Nehw'eril . . . much more advanced . . . much safer," and there was tremendous celebration on the day of its "opening."[5] Security was tight in the new district, as it was revealed later that the Relyimah had uncovered a variety of plots intended to display some of the faction's disagreement with the district.

In 5540 DE, Me'emen's only son became extremely ill and ended up passing away six months later. As a member of the Guild of Healers, Ashem was often among the first to investigate new Ages to make sure of their safety in relation to disease. As a result of his death, the Age was not approved until a cure could be found. Me'emen considered the actions of his son heroic and changed the name of the Uran District to Ashem'en a year after his death.

It was said that the death left Me'emen "deeply saddened . . . devoid of the excitement he had shown throughout his reign."[6] Many said it forced him to the Prophetess Trisari.[7] Me'emen apparently spent much time with Trisari in his last days and was able to die a content man "because of her."[8]

Me'emen died in 5549 DE at the very ripe age of 392 and choose his nephew, probably on recommendation of Trisari, to succeed him.

NOTES

1. A metallic gray stone thirty times the density of steel and the hardest of all D'ni stones.

2. Yasefe was mostly forest and provided D'ni with a good portion of its wood supply including the expensive, and rare, Yema.

3. The industrial district was formed during the reign of Needrah and served as an importation center for most outside goods.

4. The newer Ages allowed for much more experimentation with atmospheres, animal life, and energy sources.

5. From the journal of Grand Master Veshar of the Guild of Stone Miners.

6. From the journals of the Prophetess Trisari, assigned to King Me'emen.

7. It should be noted that prophetesses had been assigned to all of the Kings but, for the most part, had become nothing more than figureheads, rarely consulted.

8. From <u>Ashem</u>, written by Ramena in 5589.

Journal: King Asemlef

<u>Asemlef</u> took the throne in 5999 DE at the age of 54.

Asemlef inherited a people who were philosophically confused (The Watcher vs. Gish vs. The Great King/Tevahr), but technologically advancing (many great construction, mining, and scientific inventions), expanding within the cavern at a great rate, and moving toward diminishing the involvement of the outsiders within their culture. As well, the fighting that had scarred their past was at a minimum.[1]

This journal was discovered in the DRC field office on a D'ni rooftop, which was reached via a Linking Stone in Lower Gira.

Asemlef continued the peaceful trends by attempting to isolate no one, but instead welcoming everyone and any beliefs they might have had.

It seems he took no stance on any of the varying religious ideologies being passed around and allowed any and all religious factions equal access to property, government help, etc.

While disregarding no beliefs, he was able to hold his own, some of which were unknown to D'ni up to that point. Though never stated publicly by Asemlef, common opinion and historical records point toward numerous servants being used by Asemlef, most brought from outside Ages. More so, were the apparent challenges Asemlef held with these "servants". Details are hard to find, but it seems as though these challenges ranged from hunts, by Asemlef himself, to gladiator-style battles between the servants. It should be noted that regardless of what actions occurred, there was little public outcry against them.

Instead of philosophical or religious beliefs, Asemlef instead focused on mining expansion, construction of the new districts and offering equal opportunities of culture and social benefits to all classes. As far as outside involvement, Asemlef publicly argued that the order from his father to all of the Guilds was not realistic and that outside involvement would always be needed to some extent. Knowing the comment would anger some of the factions, he became the first King to publicly invite the more extreme factions (who wanted no outside involvement) to his palace for numerous talks on the issues.

Though no decisions were made in the meetings, the meetings themselves apparently calmed the factions and created a better overall feeling that the two could come to a decision in the future.

Around the same time, two key writers from the Writer's Guild left to join the Writers of Yahvo.[2] Up to that point, the group, who believed it was their duty to write the Perfect Age,[3] had been relatively small.

Like the Writers of Yahvo, most of the popular factions or cults of the day focused on Yahvo in one way or another. The old cults (such as The Tree and Sacred Stone) had vanished for the most part leaving way to disagreements in the beliefs of Yahvo for the most part.

Asemlef passed away in 6284 DE at the age of 339 leaving the throne to his third (and youngest) son.

NOTES

1. From <u>The Line of Kerath</u>, written by F'hal in 6985.

2. Worth mentioning as the Writers of Yahvo would eventually become one of the three largest sects in all of D'ni.

3. After the Judgment Age, most of D'ni believed one would either end up in the Perfect Age or Jakooth's Age. Obviously, most wanted to live in the Perfect Age, but there were, of course, a variety of beliefs on how that was accomplished.

Journal: King Kerath

<u>Kerath</u> took the throne in 6731 DE at the age of 54. Kerath is probably the most well known name of all the Kings, not because he was necessarily considered the best, but because he was the last. His name came to represent all of the Kings in the later years, including the renaming of the Arch of the Kings to the Arch of Kerath.

This journal was discovered in the DRC field office on a D'ni rooftop, which was reached via a Linking Stone in Lower Gira.

His mother had raised him to follow the teachings of Gish and by the time he took the throne he was believed to be a whole-hearted believer in the Followers. Because of that, and the experience of watching his father interact with his advisors, Kerath had decided from an early age that a King was no longer the correct way that D'ni should be led. At least, he argued, not until the true Great King would come.

The fact that Kerath, in a single reign, was able to convince his people that the way they had been ruled for thousands of years was wrong and should be changed should be considered nothing short of miraculous. Kerath carefully crafted his arguments as a benefit for the Guilds more than anything else. After all, he argued, "D'ni is the Guilds . . . let us be protected by their fortress and be ruled by their wisdom."[1]

It was hard for the Guilds not to support a proposal that removed the King from the highest authority and replaced him with Five Lords, Lords that would be automatically chosen from the Grand Masters of the Guilds. It gave all of the power of D'ni to the Guilds and there were only a few Grand Masters who seemed to disagree. Those few were known as faithful followers of the Great King and Ri'neref, who had always supported the role of Kings.

Fortunately, for Kerath, though his people believed a variety of different philosophical ideologies, only those who faithfully followed the original teachings of Ri'neref and the Great King were disturbed at the thought of no King. And it was the majority of D'ni who no longer followed those beliefs but instead those of Nemiya, Gish, The Watcher and various others. As a result it was a cultural impact that the public had to overcome and not a religious one.[2]

Kerath, attempting to further please the Guilds, recommended new renovations and additions to the Council Chamber and construction of a new Guild Hall, meant to celebrate the new power that would be theirs—a symbol of the new power of the Guilds and Lords and further insult to the Great King, burying his memory even further under government construction.

Construction began in 6970 DE on the new Guild Hall. There was no better symbol of the attitude of the D'ni in 6970 DE. The Tomb of the Great King was further buried under massive buildings dedicated to government and the Guilds.

By the end of his reign, Kerath had convinced a majority of D'ni of his own beliefs. Most claimed to be followers of Gish and his writings, and most viewed the outsiders as a threat. "If not now, then soon," Kerath often said.[3]

After his death, Kerath's words would be proven true with the onset of the Mee-Dis War. Outside factions would invade with attempts to destroy the Ink-Making and Book-Making Guilds and almost succeed. By the time the war would end, there would be few left who did not follow Gish and thus believe in the end of most outsider involvement. The discovery that conservative factions had led to the start of the Mee-Dis War would come much later, when it was far too late to alter the conservative trends.

Regardless, in 6977 DE Kerath abdicated the throne and gave over the power of the Kings to the first Five Lords of D'ni History. They were Lord Taeri of the Guild of Messengers, Lord Hemelah of the Guild of Healers, Lord Moleth of the Guild of Caterers, Lord Kedri of the Guild of Writers, and Lord Korenen of the Guild of Analysts. Kerath died eight years later.

The time of the Kings was over.

NOTES

1. Taken from Kerath's public speech in which he first proposed the idea.

2. From The First Five, written by Tarvis in 7000.

3. From How They Came; A Detailed Look at What Started the Mee-Dis War, by Jamen. Written in 7201.

Journal: Shomat Story

The Story of Shomat—taken from one book 43C. (We have yet to name it.)

Translation: Nick

First Draft

At the age of 121, Shomat had resided in his Palace of the Kings for twenty years. Though the palace had taken forty-five years to construct and new additions (?) had been added every year, Shomat was still not pleased with all that surrounded him. His palace was larger than any structure in the city, and the gardens of his palace were more beautiful than any other living plants that the people had ever known. But Shomat demanded more from those who created his home and his gardens.

This journal was found above a tunnel entrance in Eder Kimo, near the puffer grove. It was apparently stolen from the DRC field office on a D'ni rooftop.

Shomat sent messengers demanding that Lemash, the head (this word seems to define some kind of leader of the servants—although they never defined them as servants. Have to ask Dr. Watson) of his palace come to his gardens immediately. And Lemash obeyed. "Yes, my King, what is it that you require of me?"

"Do you see these bulbs of orange and leaves of brown that surround me?"

"Of course, my King. They are unlike any that dwell in this cavern."

"Do you see the intricate stone that surrounds me?" asked Shomat.

"Of course, again there is none like them in the cavern."

And Shomat suddenly became angry, cursing at his servants (not really servants but it'll have to do) and screaming at those in his presence.

"Who do you think that I am? Do you think I have never used the Books to see the beauties that lie outside this cavern? I have written these Books myself, even while you have seen me trained by the Grand Master! And yet you act as though I should be pleased at the beauty that now surrounds me. Beauty that comes only from this cavern, this cavern of no light, no warmth, and no color? Do you think stone and darkness are all that I require? Who do you think that I am?"

"My King, what is it that you ask of me?"

"Bring to me Grand Master Kenri. Together you will work (work in a writing sense?) with him and create for me real beauty. Roaring water. Colors beyond imagination. Living creations, not stone! These are the gardens that I demand! Now go and bring them to me."

And so Lemash went to Kenri, Grand Master of the Guild of Writers, and together they created an Age whose beauty was beyond that which any man had seen before. And together they brought their King to the Age, eight months (these are D'ni months) after his request had been made.

Shomat was pleased with all that he saw. Broad leaves of green and yellow, flowers of every color, and roaring waters of blue and turquoise like the most colorful stones of D'ni. And he promoted Lemash (as he was already head, I'm not sure his promotion but the word is fairly clear) and made Kenri his most prized Grand Master in all of D'ni. Shomat spent every day on his new Age, and he asked for more of them and he asked his architects to provide structures on these Ages.

And while this happened, Shomat's brothers continued to grow more jealous and their anger turned to rage. They had not been invited to live in the palace of their brother and now, though multitudes of common citizens were invited to the gardens of Shomat, never once were they allowed to visit. And their hearts burned toward their King and brother.

So it was that Shomat was sitting alone in his Garden Age when two creatures approached him. Though they resembled men, they walked on their arms and legs and moved quickly. Shomat was frightened upon seeing the creatures and immediately called for his guards. The creatures ran from the guards but Shomat ordered his guards to follow them and the guards obeyed. It was not until the next day that they returned. They claimed they had seen a city with hundreds of these creatures living in it, conversing with one another, and organizing armies. These armies lived inside of the Garden Age of Shomat. And Shomat was very afraid.

Shomat ordered the men who had seen the village to be put in prison (not sure if Book or physical prison) for what they saw. And he called his most trusted advisor (?) Lemash to his residence in the city. Upon hearing of the creatures and their organization, Lemash too was frightened.

"We have no choice but to burn the Book," Lemash recommended. "You know this Age is not ours, if it is already inhabited. You know the rules of our Writing, and of our Books, and of our people."

But Shomat's heart was not moved by the words of Lemash and he grew more angry and enraged. "The world was created by me, for me. If there are others who exist, they will have to be killed. It is D'ni now."

So Shomat ordered for his brothers to be brought into his palace and he informed them of his dilemma. Shomat asked his brothers if they would kill those who lived on his Garden Ages and he bribed them with talk of power and authority. And so they agreed even though they hated their brother.

And the brothers of Shomat traveled to the Age, and went to the creatures to destroy them. But in talking with the creatures they became convinced that the creatures should not be killed but instead they should be used to destroy their brother. And so they devised a plan to kill their brother, the King.

While Shomat waited in his Palace in the city, his brothers appeared to him.

"We have finished," they announced. "The creatures are all dead."

Shomat was pleased to hear such words from his brothers and on the outside he showed love to them. "My brothers, I have done much wrong to you. There have been many times that I have not treated you like even those who work in my palace. And I am sorry for these actions. But today you have proven that you do not hold anger like I do. You are better than me. You have shown me favor and so I ask you to accept what I have to offer you. Please accept this gift."

And Shomat gave his brothers a Linking Book. Its pages were filled with descriptions of beauty and life, like Shomat's own Garden Age.

"And it will be kept here in this palace where you will live now."

Filled with pleasure, and forgetting their hate for Shomat, his brothers went to the Age quickly. And it was there that they died thinking that they had fooled their brother. Shomat burned the Book in his own fire, forever erasing his brothers and their deceit from his mind.

And Shomat ordered the Grand Master to change his Garden Age so that those who lived there would die. And Kenri obeyed the King even though he knew it was wrong. And his life was filled with turmoil until he died.

But Shomat, though he did what was wrong, continued to live and pursue all that he wanted.

The story continues but it seemed a good point to stop. I'd like to go over this a few more times with some better translators—maybe even Dr. Watson. I filled in a lot of words as best I could for now.

The DRC welcomes you...

The largest archaeological restoration in history is underway. Deep beneath the surface, the ancient city of D'ni is being restored and you can be a part of it. Stand in awe of the Arch of Kerath. Climb the ancient Great Stairs. Explore beyond the ruins to remarkable ages. The DRC is looking for volunteers.

Join now!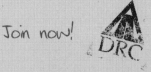

Join the restoration!

"We stand on the edge of a precipice of discovery and enlightenment."

Dr. Watson

www.drcsite.org